BY THE WAY®

THOUGHTS FOR YOUR DAY

PAUL DEVANTIER

To Lois, with
best wishes in Christ!

Thoughts for your day based
upon messages from the popular
BY THE WAY *radio program*

COVER PHOTO

Little Spider Lake, Arbor Vitae, Wisconsin

I've always been fond of lakes – summer swimming and water sports, winter activities when the lakes are completely frozen and covered in snow, watching the seasons change with the beautiful fall colors of the trees surrounding the lake and the green of spring as nature comes back to life. But there's a more significant reason for the photo. For me, it is a simple image of tranquility, quietude, and peacefulness. A familiar Scripture passage (and a favorite of mine) is this: *"Be still, and know that I am God"* (Psalm 46:9). In its original use, God, through the Psalmist, is warning those who oppose Him to stop resisting Him and battling against Him. The words also remind us that our God is, indeed, the one and only God of the universe who will never be defeated. It's a bit like saying, "take a breath, be quiet, relax, as it were, and know how great your everlasting God is!" Too seldom do I do that, and you may admit that such is true for you, as well. It's in the quiet moments of our lives that we can meditate on the wondrous grace, mercy, and blessings of a loving God in Jesus Christ. It could be while reading God's Word. It could be while gazing in solitude at some of God's marvelous creation. It could be at night before fading off to sleep. It could be in the midst of a hectic world when we turn things off for just a brief time to communicate with God in prayer – a word of thanks and praise, a call for help or forgiveness, a plea for comfort or guidance.

Being still can be a great experience. It can take us back to what is most important. It can lead us to the remembrance of a God that cares for us at all times, a God who demonstrated his eternal compassion for us in the person of Jesus Christ, a God Almighty in whose strong, yet tender and loving arms, we reside.

It is my prayer that the BY THE WAY program and the messages in this book provide an opportunity to be still, for just a short time, to dwell on God's goodness and, perhaps, to be reminded of how he would have us live as his dear children. It may be at the office, at school, in the car, working around the house, or sitting on a lake shore in the early morning hour's stillness peering at the gentle mist rising from the lake. Wherever it might be that a BY THE WAY message reaches you, may it help you in just a small way to be still, to know better your marvelous God, and to love Him more completely.

INTRODUCTION

"THANKS FOR BEING THERE AS PART OF OUR DAILY ROUTINE!"

(From a listener)

Listeners throughout the United States and beyond have come to rely on a brief message each day that points them to a loving God in Jesus Christ – a message that gives them just a simple, understandable thought to take with them. BY THE WAY offers insights and encouragement. It points to those things most important in life. It helps make dark days brighter, and bright days even better. It reminds listeners of whose they are – children of a loving Heavenly Father.

Since its beginning as a radio program, BY THE WAY has reached out in a variety of other ways, as well. It has been used in schools, hospitals, and nursing homes. In recent decades, the Internet has made it easily available for anyone at any time of the day. Also, three BY THE WAY books have been published prior to this one. They have become devotional resources for use in many settings.

IT'S ONE OF A KIND...

And that, of course, has been said about many things. In the case of BY THE WAY, there are a number of things that qualify for that description.

In broadcasting, few programs have been consistently on the air for more years than BY THE WAY. The program began in 1956, sponsored by radio station KFUO in St. Louis, Missouri, the world's oldest religious radio station. Initially called *Portals of Prayer*, its name was later changed to BY THE WAY, yet its purpose remained the same.

Added to the record span of years is the fact that the program was produced for broadcast seven days a week, 365 days a year. While other broadcasts in the history of radio have spanned many years, few, if any, have been blessed to reach listeners every single day since 1956. Unlike most radio programs, the hosts (speakers) have never been fully identified on the air. From the very first days of the program, the message, not the speaker, was to be the principal focus. Also unlike most radio programs of its type, at no time has the program been used to solicit financial support or promote fund-raising endeavors.

"An Inspiring Message Today. Thank You."

(From a listener)

Listeners to By The Way have been very kind in their response to the program. Since the program is broadcast on quite a number of radio stations and through the Internet worldwide, listener comments come from many locations. The notes and e-mails reveal how By The Way messages have made a difference in people's lives:

- *By The Way is an inspiration in our everyday life.*
- *May God continue to inspire and uplift you as you inspire and uplift all of us listeners to whom God has spoken through your words.*
- *Sure enjoy you on the radio as I wake up every morning.*
- *I am blessed to hear it each day as I am driving to work.*
- *Keep sending the messages.*
- *We have By The Way as a link on our church Web site. I enjoy the positive, short messages often. Thanks for developing them and for their easy use.*
- *I was so happy to locate your Web site. So often you say just what I need for the day. My faith gets a boost daily.*

Radio stations send notes, too:

- *Hi Paul and thank you for bringing us the By The Way program.*
- *Bless you! You and By The Way are a pleasant part of our broadcast day. Thank you.*
- *I am trying to acquire clearance to air your short form feature…we are excited to air it.*

"It Is A Blessing To Hear Your Voice"

(From a listener)

The voice that has become familiar to so many has been the voice of By The Way since 1974. As of this printing, he has shared some 14,500 messages. From time to time, he will refer to himself on the program as "Paul," and he is always delighted when listeners write "Dear Paul." But Paul would be quick to add that he is just the messenger – one who is privileged to share strong, eternal, and flawless truths of God.

Radio has always been important to Paul. He is thankful to God for the gift of radio. He came to love radio as a very young child. He recalls being amazed at what the small crystal set he built in Boy Scouts could do. He remembers listening to a small transistor radio under the covers of his bed at night. He saw radio as a great and mysterious gift, and he still does.

A radio station in his hometown hired him as a radio announcer shortly after he graduated from high school. He worked for a number of radio stations during his college and seminary studies. That background prepared him for work in his professional ministry related to Christian communications – radio, television, satellite, Internet, publications, etc. BY THE WAY has been one of the ways for him to combine his love for radio with his desire to communicate the love of God in Jesus Christ.

Paul's voice and his style have been described as "calming, friendly, sincere, and reassuring." Listeners often say things such as *"Your messages are very uplifting and calming."* Also, they comment on his approach. *"You have a unique way of saying a lot in a brief message."* And *"I am always amazed at how you manage to marry ideas in living to the Bible."* Of course, what brings the greatest joy to Paul are listener comments such as this one: *"I listen to you everyday. You've really changed my life."*

Paul is married to his wife, Ellen. They have five children, and have been very active in adoption, foster care and child welfare activities. Frequently you will hear Paul talk about one of his favorite subjects – children.

ANOTHER BOOK

This is the fourth BY THE WAY book. The one prior to this one was published in 2007. Included in this edition are just a small number of the 14,500-plus messages that Paul has recorded for broadcast prior to the date of this publication. The messages cover a variety of subjects. They are typical of the kind of simple, down-to-earth thoughts regularly shared through the broadcasts.

It is Paul's prayer that the contents of this book will help readers, if only in a small way, to see clearly the grace and mercy of Almighty God. He prays the messages will be helpful to many who strive to live their lives in God-pleasing ways.

A Very Special Thank You

Paul wishes to express his deep appreciation for all the helpers who have made his job easier and more enjoyable. Those who have been part of the production and distribution of By The Way are grateful for the radio stations and other media outlets that have chosen to include By The Way in their schedules. Thanks go to KFUO Radio for its long-term support, to Village Lutheran Church in Ladue, Missouri, for its assistance, and to congregations and other entities that include By The Way on their Web sites. Also, Paul thanks the many who have been kind encouragers to him through the years. As By The Way begins a new phase in its history, he offers sincere thanks to those who provided valuable initial leadership to launch the new By The Way organization. Those who provided the support, counsel, and vision for an ongoing and expanded By The Way ministry include Eugene and Linda Lehr, Pete and Mary Ellen Peck, and Robert and (the sainted) Lori Duesenberg. The Peck family is thanked for its strong encouragement to produce this By The Way book.

Today By The Way is produced and distributed by the incorporated By The Way ministry. By The Way is supported entirely through voluntary contributions.

It has been a special joy for me to assist with the production of this book. Best wishes to all those who use it!

Nancy Olson
By The Way Book Project Director

By The Way

Thoughts For Your Day

TABLE OF CONTENTS

SECTION I – THE CHRISTIAN LIFE

TABLE OF CONTENTS

TABLE OF CONTENTS

TABLE OF CONTENTS

TABLE OF CONTENTS

SECTION IV – HOLIDAYS AND SPECIAL OCCASIONS

TABLE OF CONTENTS

Unless otherwise noted, all Scripture references are from the ESV – English Standard Version.

SECTION I

THE CHRISTIAN LIFE

THOUGHTS FOR YOUR DAY

PERSONAL MESSENGER

By the way, how do you deliver personal messages these days? Many of us remember the days when what we now call "snail mail" was still *the* most widely used method. And old land line telephones, too. Then came voice message systems and cell phones. And then e-mail. And then texting on cell phones became very popular. Who knows what all of the next popular methods might entail.

What remains *most* important is the message itself. And the most effective way to package a message is the same today as it has always been – in the form of a person. No communication device will ever be more effective than a real, live, human being. Perhaps that's why God chose to send His Son to earth to tell people directly of His Father's glory and His Father's plan for all eternity. And perhaps that is why He calls upon the likes of us to be powerful and personal "messages" to those around us.

Prayer thought: In your Holy Word (I Peter 2:9), Almighty God, you called us "chosen" and said that we are people called to "proclaim" you who called us "out of darkness" into your "marvelous light." Help us to be messengers for Jesus. In his name. Amen.

Hearing His Voice

The voice is a powerful instrument. Hearing a familiar and friendly voice can mean a lot, and it starts early in life. It's actually true, we're told, that a child still in the womb, becomes very familiar with mother's voice, and that familiarity leads to a strong connection to that voice once the child is born. There are so many voices in our world, aren't there. Some can be soothing, friendly, and kind. Some are sharp and unsettling. Some tempt. Some seek to sell. Some speak the truth. Others do not. We all hear many of those voices, but what are the most meaningful in your life?

Jesus once said, *"My sheep hear my voice, and I know them, and they follow me"* (John 10:27). What a wonderful voice. It's the voice we hear as we study God's Word. It's a voice of love, forgiveness, comfort, assurance, hope, and promise. It's a great voice…and it's a voice worth following.

Prayer thought: How blessed we are, Lord Jesus, to know your loving voice through the gift of faith in you that we have received. Yours is the best of all voices. How fortunate we are to hear it and follow it. Amen.

WORDS THAT REMAIN

Back in 1793, President George Washington delivered his second inaugural address. It contained only 133 words – a little shorter than one of these BY THE WAY messages. That is certainly not typical of many speeches today. But often, it's the short, concise thought that is remembered.

When President Franklin Roosevelt delivered his inauguration address in 1933, it was not remembered for either its brevity or its considerable length. The address was delivered in the midst of the Great Depression and is remembered for one simple phrase that has been quoted perhaps millions of times since. The simple phrase of President Roosevelt is this: "We have nothing to fear but fear itself."

So many of the words of Jesus were brief, to the point, and memorable. Here's an example: *"And you shall love the Lord your God with all your heart…soul… strength, and mind and your neighbor as yourself"* (Luke 10:27).

Prayer thought: Thank you, Lord Jesus, for speaking important truths to us in ways that we can understand. Help us to remember them and to live them for your sake. Amen.

JOY

So, are you happy today? Are you joyful today? You might think those two questions are asking essentially the same thing. But they are actually quite different.

We all experience situations and circumstances that are not happy ones. So your response to the question about happiness may be to say, "No, actually, I'm not very happy today. There are things in my life that are not necessarily happy things." But that doesn't mean you are left without joy. Joy is that inner sense of complete trust in God. He is in control. He cares. Nothing will happen to us without His knowledge, and His plan for us for all eternity is an excellent one, indeed. So really, joy is something we can always have, despite circumstances that detract from our happiness.

A Psalm in the Bible says it very well when it says that in the presence of the Lord is *"fullness of joy"* (Psalm 16:11). For joy, stay closely connected to God.

 Prayer thought: Lord God, open me to discover and experience the joy you promised, even in situations that may not seem joyful. In Jesus Christ, with your gift of faith, I can know joy. Amen.

DON'T BE SHY

By the way, do you pray? If you are a Christian, you surely do. You may pray familiar prayers such as the Lord's Prayer. You may pray other prayers you know such as meal time prayers. But when you find yourself in a situation where a familiar prayer doesn't seem quite appropriate, how do you express your heart feelings and needs to God? And in situations, how bold are you?

Being too bold may be like trying to twist God's arm. That may not be appropriate for a Christian approaching God in all humility. But we're told in Scripture that God is fully capable of things we would consider impossible. In the New Testament book of Ephesians we are told that our loving God *"…is able to do far more abundantly than all that we ask or think"* (Ephesians 3:20). So, don't be shy when talking with God. Remember, He is capable of far more than we could possibly imagine!

Prayer thought: Almighty God, how quickly and how often we underestimate your power. We need to remember that there are no limits on your capability and no limits on your love for us in Jesus Christ, our Savior. Amen.

DRESS YOUR BEST

A fairly common complaint of folks these days is that their clothes start to shrink. They just don't fit as well as they once did. No wonder there are so many diet plans available today.

Well, it's nice to know that some clothing will always fit. In the Bible we are told to *"...put on the new self, created to be like God in true righteousness and holiness"* (Ephesians 4:24). Faith in Jesus Christ leads Christians to want to be like Him, to follow His example, to do those things that are pleasing to Him. That's what it means to "put on the new self." Consequently, we don't put on anger or bitterness or jealousy or pride or a whole host of other things that do not "fit" Christians. Rather, we put on kindness and compassion and forgiveness and love and humility and patience and all sorts of other things that will always "fit" perfectly.

Prayer thought: Lord Jesus, you have offered us newness that reflects your love and holiness to those around us. With your help, we can put on that newness. Lead us to wear it for your sake. Amen.

THREE IMPORTANT WORDS

We're all acquainted with the frequently-mentioned importance in business of "location, location, location." Of course there are many things important to business, but location is certainly one of them. When it comes to the area of attitude and behavior for human beings, it might be appropriate to say that three of the most important things are kindness…kindness…and kindness.

There are, of course, many important things for each of us as we live out our lives. But kindness is a good one to consider. We may not see as much of it in our world as we would like. That is all the more reason for us to practice it.

The Apostle Paul in the Bible, who was so dramatically touched by the kindness of his loving God, said it well: *"Be kind to one another, tenderhearted, forgiving each other, as God in Christ forgave you"* (Ephesians 4:32).

Kindness…kindness…kindness. Three words worth remembering today!

Prayer thought: Dear Jesus, we may be able to reflect your love and kindness in the ways we relate to those around us this day. As you give us chances to do that, let us not forget the importance of kindness. In your name. Amen.

WALK THE TALK

The Apostle John was an old man when he wrote the letter that is recorded in the New Testament of the Bible – the letter in which he said, *"My little children, let us not love in word or talk but in deed and in truth"* (I John 3:18). No doubt John had heard many loving words from many people. We have, too. And, perhaps, we have concluded, as John did, that words are cheap and that love is best expressed in deeds.

It's true, isn't it! Talking about love – speaking loving words – is much easier than demonstrating love. That is particularly true when it comes to the "unlovable" – those who upset us, those who are beneath us, those whom we might consider our enemies. You'll probably encounter some of those people today. Remember the words of John. Remember the example of Christ…and with His help, love, not just with words, but with deeds, as well.

Prayer thought: It is true, Heavenly Father, that talk can be cheap. May our faith in Jesus Christ always move us to not just talk of love but to show it to those around us, for Jesus' sake. Amen.

Lost It By Neglect

I never intentionally sought to let my marriage fall apart," said the person now facing divorce. "It just kind of slipped away." So many of us could say something similar about important relationships in our lives – "they just kind of slipped away." How about close relationships with children? "We didn't mean to be so distant from our children, but somehow they just slipped away." Or perhaps your faith just slipped away. It was important when you were younger, but today you find yourself very distant from God.

Neglect can cause a lot of heartache and regret. It's not that we consciously sought to be separated from family, friends, or even from our faith in Jesus Christ. It's conceivable that those separations just happened through neglect.

What is it in your life that is truly worth preserving? Don't neglect those things. Ask God to help you give them the attention they deserve.

Prayer thought: Lord Jesus, open my eyes to important treasures that I am neglecting. I need to know that precious gifts require care and I need to give them careful attention. Jesus, give me the strength and insight to do so. Amen.

LIVING THIS DAY

There's a phrase I've heard that captures in a few words a significant truth. It's something to the effect of "Life happens while we're planning for other things." As human beings, we do spend quite a bit of time and energy hoping, wishing, planning and dreaming about the future. And sometimes that means we miss what is happening in the here and now. It's good to dream. It's good to look forward. But it is also good to fully experience and appreciate what is happening in our lives at this moment in time.

This day, and every day, Jesus Christ is in our lives – loving us, embracing us, extending His care to us, and giving us reasons to celebrate and to be grateful. If we will but pay attention, we will see the wonders that exist in our lives today. While we have dreams of wonders for tomorrow, let's not miss those that surround us today. Thanks, Lord, for being with us at this very time and in this very place.

Prayer thought: Indeed, Lord Jesus, you have blessed us in so many ways. Open our eyes to see all the blessings that surround us this day so that we might appreciate them and thank you for them. In your name. Amen.

KEEP ON SHOVELING

If you are currently raising children or if you have had that experience earlier in your life, you know what a busy and hectic time it can be. There's so much to think about and do. We can't get it all done. In our home there was a little saying that hung on the wall close to the children's bedrooms – something my wife cross-stitched. It said "Cleaning the house while the kids are still growing is like shoveling the snow while it's still snowing."

It's true in many areas of life. Some jobs are just never completely done.

Loving and forgiving are good examples. As long as we live on this earth, there will be the need to love and forgive those around us. Jesus taught us how to do that. Sin and separation and temptation will just keep "snowing down upon us," as it were. Yet, we can thank God we have His strength, love, forgiveness, and help as we seek to "clear a path" that can lead to happy and blessed relationships.

Prayer thought: Almighty God, you declared to us in your Word that we should not "…grow weary in doing good" (II Thessalonians 3:13). As long as we live we will have opportunities to do good to those around us. Help us do so for Jesus' sake.

MY FAULT

I t's my fault. I'm sorry." That's a sentiment not too common in our world today. It's easier to say and more common to hear "It's their fault, or my friends' fault, or my parents' fault, or my boss's fault, or the government's fault," and so on. Benjamin Franklin echoed the thought when he said: "How few there are who have courage enough to own their faults, or resolution enough to mend them."

As Franklin observed, we have to admit and own our faults before we even have the inclination to change, to make amends. The good news of God's grace – His undeserved love through the life, death, and resurrection of Jesus – is fully appreciated only when we know how much we need it. When we come to grips with our sins and seek forgiveness, then we can fully celebrate God's goodness.

It's my fault, God. For Jesus' sake, forgive me, and then lead me to change my sinful ways.

Prayer thought: Eternal Father, how clear is your call – "Repent, therefore, and turn back, that your sins may be blotted out" (Acts 3:19). For Jesus' sake, help us always to admit that we are responsible for our sins. Amen.

THE BUSYNESS TRAP

It's a "hurry-up" world, isn't it! Places to go, things to do. But if you look closely, you may just conclude that a lot of the activity is really meaningless. Does it make us stronger as human beings? Does it help those around us? Does it bring us closer to our loving God? Or is it just a lot of activity of little true value? As one person described it, "I am so busy doing nothing that I can't find time to do much of anything."

Not everything we do is of great significance. Some things are simply necessary as part of life. Still, God would have us devote some of our time and energy to those things that He tells us are important. As you go through your day today, ask yourself, "Could I, in some way, make better use of the precious time and abilities God has given me?"

 Prayer thought: Lord God, you counseled us saying "Look carefully then how you walk…making the best use of time…" (Ephesians 5:15, 16). The time you have given us is a gift. Help us to use it wisely. In Jesus' name. Amen.

GOD'S PLAN OR MINE?

By the way, how well organized are you? Are you able to find things in the kitchen or in the office or in the attic quickly and easily? If so, you may be the exception. I tried recently to organize some of the many things I have retained through the years. I was not completely successful. I didn't really have the time to devote to the task and all sorts of other things continued to get in the way. I've discovered through the years that my system is a bit like office filing. It's supposed to be an orderly system, but ends up as a system for misplacing important papers.

Some things can be organized. Some cannot. When a spouse or child or friend needs your help or some of your time, if may not fit your "system." Still, it may be the very best use of your time. Today, be open to the unexpected opportunities that come your way. What you do for others may not always be part of your plan, but may, indeed, be part of God's plan.

Prayer thought: I don't always see the opportunities to reach out in love to others, Lord Jesus, because I am too busy with other things. Open my eyes to ways I can respond to the needs of others. In your name. Amen

HUG-POWER

She met me at the door when I arrived home from work. I could tell she wasn't very happy. "Dad," said my 9-year-old daughter, in a drawn-out and somber tone, "you didn't give me a hug this morning."

She was correct. I had left for work early, while she was still asleep. I knew I was in trouble, but she was forgiving. I said I was sorry. We did a double hug to make up for the one missed and everything was OK again. That's quite some years ago. But the problem my 9-year-old had was easily solved.

It certainly would be nice if all problems could come to a positive resolution. But even for the tough ones, a hug, or a smile, or a phone call, or just a kind word can go a long way. There is someone who may need one of those from you today. Remembering how God always offers His love to us, why not send some expression of love and concern to someone near you today.

 Prayer thought: Lord Jesus, it says so often in Scripture that you had concern for, and showed kindness to, others. Help us always to follow your example. Amen.

Is It Possible?

I t's impossible!" You've probably said that at one time or another. We look at the challenge, the opportunity, the chance to fix something that is broken and we conclude "it's impossible."

Well, many things in this world are. But sometimes, saying "it's impossible" is a conclusion that gets us off the hook. If it is impossible, I no longer have to worry too much about it and I don't have to be too disappointed that it can't be fixed, improved, or resolved.

What about changing the world? Impossible. What about overcoming poverty? Impossible. What about fighting crime? Impossible. What about changing attitudes and behaviors that are hurting so many people? Impossible. What about living your faith in such a way that it really changes the lives of others. Impossible. Well, don't be too sure. It's been said that "Every noble work is at first impossible." And, of course, with God on your side, noble works are, indeed, possible!

Prayer thought: Loving Lord Jesus, when you were on earth you promised that "...with God, all things are possible" (Matthew 19:26). When I face what seems impossible, help me look to God. In your name I pray. Amen.

LOSING TO GAIN

We have to check your credit score." Any time you seek to purchase something on credit, you will likely hear that phrase. I understand why that is necessary, but it still bothers me a bit. My word is no longer good enough. What we are worth on earth in terms of possessions, resources, and earning potential means a lot. These things determine how you are judged. But what about our "heavenly" value?

Ultimately, for each of us, earthly possessions will have no value at all. In the final analysis, it is only the heavenly possessions that have real lasting value. Recognizing the one, true God and having faith in His Son, Jesus Christ, are possessions in God's safe keeping that *will* last. Martin Luther said it this way: "I have held many things in my hands, and I have lost them all; but whatever I have placed in God's hands, that I still possess."

 Prayer thought: Heavenly Father, because of Jesus Christ, "...we know that if the tent that is our earthly home is destroyed, we have a building from God, a house not made with hands, eternal in the heavens" (II Corinthians 5:1). How blessed we are! Amen.

KEEP IT SIMPLE

I have a little sign in my office that says "Eschew obfuscation." Those two words are just a cleverly complex and amusing way of saying "stay away from things that are complex and confusing." Another definition would be just this: "Keep it simple." We don't always need big words. Sometimes we may need the more sophisticated, technical words and sometimes they may be absolutely essential. But often times keeping it simple is just the best way to communicate.

Jesus spoke to people in ways they could understand. His parables and down-to-earth illustrations connected with people. He was not interested in impressing people with fancy speech and sophisticated logic. And he acted accordingly. I guess we've all known people who can wow others with great logic, but their actions do not always match. As some wise person has said, "People will be more impressed by the depth of your conviction than the height of your logic." The Lord will help us understand, so that we can keep our speech understandable...and our actions sincere.

Prayer thought: Dear Father, you have blessed us so we can say with St. John, "We know that the Son of God has come and has given us understanding so that we may know him who is true...Jesus Christ..." (I John 5:20). Thank you, in Jesus' name. Amen.

GREATNESS IN HUMILITY

No doubt you have worked with and have come to know a lot of people during your lifetime. Some may have inspired you with their intellect. Some may have had great work ethics that impressed you. Some may have had a number of advanced degrees. Some have been real entrepreneurs. You've known people with a lot of impressive characteristics. I have, too. But the one that has stood out more than many of the rest for me is humility. That, it seems, is a bit hard to find in our world today. It is not necessarily celebrated as a positive personal characteristic.

When Jesus was on earth, He spoke of the *greatness* of humility. Humility, according to Him, was an outstanding characteristic. Of course, that doesn't mean the world in which we live treasures humility. It may be just the opposite. But then, it's good to remind ourselves that the Lord's opinion is always superior to that of the world.

BY THE WAY
THOUGHTS FOR YOUR DAY

Prayer thought: Lord Jesus, you said: "Whoever exalts himself will be humbled, and whoever humbles himself will be exalted" (Matthew 23:12). each us always to prize humility. Amen.

HARD TO BE HUMBLE

In the previous message the virtue of humility was mentioned. Now a little follow up – an amusing, but pointed, fable that reminds us of the risks of self-centeredness and pride. Here it is:

There were two ducks and a frog living in a farmer's pond. They actually became friends and enjoyed one another's company. As the summer wore on, the pond began to dry up. That was not a problem for the ducks, but it could be for the frog. How could he get to another pond, perhaps miles away? Well, the frog suggested he could hold on to a stick that the ducks would carry between them as they flew to another pond. As they took off with the frog grasping the stick in his mouth, the farmer saw them and said, "How clever! I wonder who thought of that." To which the frog opened his mouth to say "I did." And that was the end of the frog.

O Lord, teach me humility!

Prayer thought: Oh God, you told us in Scripture that "Pride ends in destruction; humility ends in honor" (Proverbs 18:12 TLB). Help us choose to live lives of humility. In Jesus' name. Amen.

WALLS THAT DIVIDE

When the Berlin Wall was constructed in the early 1960s, no doubt those who had it built had plans for it to exist for generations. It was clearly designed to keep those who lived in East Germany remaining in East Germany.

As many real and figurative walls do, the Berlin Wall separated friends and families. It was a monument to the ability of an ideology and a ruling class of people to control the lives of others. But ultimately, the wall came tumbling down.

In all of our lives there are walls – not of the brick and mortar type – but walls that separate us from others. There are attitudes and prejudices and fears and misinformation. Some walls for our protection from evil may be good to keep, but others that keep us from doing what God would have us do in our world need to come down. Are there walls separating you from being all that God would have you to be?

Prayer thought: Heavenly Father, lead us to recognize those barriers in our lives that keep us from reaching out to others and doing those things you would have us do for ourselves and for others that will strengthen our relationship with Jesus. Amen.

PEOPLE LIKE US

By the way, do some people really upset you? Most of us could probably provide at least a small list of those people. Do you think there are some people who don't deserve to be forgiven? If so, you're right! Some people just don't deserve kindness and mercy, and they certainly don't deserve to be forgiven. For example, people like me…and you.

Never mind other people. What about us? We all offend others. And none of us deserves to be forgiven. When we seek forgiveness from our merciful God, He does forgive. Not because we deserve forgiveness, but because of His great love and His everlasting concern for us. Not because we deserve forgiveness, but because Jesus won it for us and offers it to us as a gift.

Let's dispense with revenge and "get even" attitudes that result when we believe others should not be forgiven. Then let us forgive others as we have been forgiven.

Prayer thought: Lord Jesus, we know your prayer that asks you to "forgive us our trespasses as we forgive those who trespass against us." Lead us to not just speak those words but to put them into practice. In your name. Amen.

THOSE WE'VE NEVER MET

If you know anything about Washington, D.C. or have been there, you know that there are many memorials. And some, like the World War II Memorial, took a long time to come into existence. Another example is the Korean War Veterans Memorial that was dedicated 42 years after the war ended. One of the plaques at the memorial has these words: "Our nation honors her sons and daughters who answered a call to defend a country they never knew and a people they never met." Of course, those words could relate to a variety of conflicts in which the United States has been engaged.

When I first saw these words, I couldn't help but think of some of the ways Christian men and women, boys and girls reach out in prayer and with gifts of support for those in places they have never visited, and for people they have never met – the hungry, alienated, fatherless, oppressed, war weary, and hopeless. The opportunities for doing exactly that still exist and I pray you might respond.

Prayer thought: You expressed your love and concern for ALL people, Lord Jesus. Teach us how to follow your example so that we can help reach even those we do not know with your love. Amen.

NO COMPROMISE

By the way, are you a compromiser? If so, you are held in rather high esteem in our culture today. Compromise is so often held up as a great virtue. If we can't reach consensus on issues, then we should compromise in order to resolve debated matters.

Compromise may make you a bit nervous. It does me. It can be good. But some things are sacred and should not be compromised. For example, the value of life, honesty, concern for others, care for my loved ones and the less fortunate, what God has said in the Bible. I'm sure I could be criticized for not being willing to compromise on these things. Someone might say, "You can't possibly believe everything in the Bible. Let's compromise and simply state that it is a nice book with some good tips for living."

Some things are sacred, including those things taught us by Jesus Christ. On these things, we should never compromise.

Prayer thought: Heavenly Father, let us never forsake or weaken the truths you have made so clear to us in your Holy Word. In Jesus' name. Amen.

LIKE A CHILD

By the way, what is it that MAKES your day? An unexpected gift? A day without conflict in the family or at the office? A good grade on a test? Lower food or gasoline prices? Your favorite meal or dessert?

My mother had a neatly stitched and framed saying hanging on a wall in her house when she was still here on this earth. It said, "My day is complete. I heard a child laugh." Few things would bring more joy to her life than being around children who were playing and having a good time. Her concern and her love for the next generation were always apparent.

So much of what we consider pleasure is simply here today, gone tomorrow. What we invest in the next generation, however, is lasting. Jesus took time for the little ones. He encouraged us to have faith like theirs. Find a laughing child today, and let that child inspire you!

Prayer thought: Lord Jesus, when the disciples asked you who is the greatest in the Kingdom of heaven, you pointed to a child. (Matthew 18:1-4) Help us to have a childlike faith and to love the little ones around us. We pray in your name. Amen.

NEEDED: WISDOM

By the way, when was the last time you prayed for wisdom? We all need a lot of it. Wisdom has been described as "the quality that keeps you from getting into situations where you need it."

Many of us have, from time to time, looked back on things we've done in our lives – perhaps something we did many years ago or, perhaps, something we did just yesterday – and said, "How dumb that was. If only I had chosen a better course of action." Unfortunately, we often appreciate the value of wisdom only after it is too late. Wisdom leads us to choose those things that are pleasing to God. In the Old Testament book of Proverbs are these words: *I have taught you the way of wisdom; I have led you in the paths of uprightness* (Proverbs 4:11).

Wisdom, as taught to us by our loving God, leads us to do what is pleasing to Him. Pray for wisdom…and then practice it!

 Prayer thought: All knowing God, how badly we need to learn wisdom. We can learn through your Word. We can observe the power of wisdom in the life and ministry of Jesus Christ. Help us put into practice the wisdom you teach us, for Jesus' sake. Amen.

GRATEFUL GIVING

When it comes to giving, someone suggested that "If you continually give you will continually have." That's true, but it is important to understand the best meaning of that phrase.

Those who are motivated to give seldom do it so that they will get a big return. That would be like stock market giving. But those motivated to give because of their gratitude for what God has given to them, will "have" things even more valuable than possessions. My father frequently said that "the more you shovel it out, the more the Lord shovels it in…and the Lord has a bigger shovel." The Lord does give material blessings to selfless givers, but what is more significant to them is the satisfaction in knowing their gifts are helping others, that they are doing what pleases God, and that, because of what Jesus Christ did for them, there is great peace and joy in loving their neighbors.

Prayer thought: Lord Jesus, when you were on earth you spoke to your disciples saying "…give and it will be given to you. Good measure, pressed down, shaken together, running over…" (Luke 6:38). Bless the gifts we give for your sake. Amen.

ENGAGED

By the way, do you attend worship services? Let me ask the question a bit differently: Do you engage in worship? Not to quibble over language, but there is a difference. Many people go to church, at least occasionally, and are bystanders. They "attend" a worship service, but don't really "engage" in worship.

Christians seek to actively engage in worship of their Lord and Savior, Jesus Christ…and the practice is not confined to a church building. You are worshipping God every time you resist evil and choose to do what is pleasing to God. You worship when you reach out to help others in Jesus' name. You worship when you study God's Word and speak to God in prayer. You worship when you look around you and whisper a heart-felt "thanks, Lord" for all the blessings He daily brings into you life. There are so many ways to engage in worship.

May you worship often…in a church, too.

Prayer thought: As you, Lord God, have encouraged us: "Therefore, let us be grateful for receiving a kingdom that cannot be shaken, and thus let us offer to God acceptable worship…" (Hebrews 12:28). In Jesus' name. Amen.

NEW MEANS, OLD MESSAGE

It's true - there's nothing new about effective tools of Satan. He has always had effective tools and people have always given in to his various means of temptation. Today, it seems, there are more temptations than ever before - books, magazines, television programs, Internet material, and so many things that circulate through social networking. So, there may be some new tools, but Satan's objective remains the same.

Fortunately, there are others with tools, as well, who have some excellent objectives. There is so much that is good and wholesome. There are excellent books and magazines and Internet sites. Reading, listening, viewing, and the way we spend our time influence our thinking and living. The people with whom we associate do, too. I pray God might help all of us, following the example of Christ, to choose those things and those people in life that fill our minds and our hearts with good things pleasing to Him.

Prayer thought: Lord God, fill our minds with thoughts pleasing to you and thoughts fashioned by our faith in the Lord Jesus Christ so that we can fight the assaults of Satan. In Jesus' name. Amen

DISAGREEABLE DISAGREEING

By the way, are you a person who is not particularly fond of controversy? You're not alone. Conflicts can be truly draining, but they are impossible to avoid. Dissention, discord, and divisiveness are everywhere - in politics, in families, in communities, even in churches.

Philip Melanchthon, an associate of the Reformer Martin Luther some 500 years ago told the parable of a war between wolves and dogs. The wolves were afraid because of the large number of dogs. They sent a spy to learn more about the behavior of the dogs. When the wolf spy returned he reported that there were, indeed, many dogs. But they were all snapping at each other. So the wolf spy concluded that the dogs may hate wolves, but they appear to hate each other just as much.

On this earth, we may never be able to avoid controversy and conflict. Still, with God's help, let's strive to find ways to deal with the disagreements we may have with others…and to do so without "snapping."

Prayer thought: Dear God, you have given to Christians "…the ministry of reconciliation…" (II Corinthians 5:18). For Jesus' sake, lead us to turn away from unholy conflict. Amen.

HARD QUESTIONS

You've probably heard the expression that "there is no such thing as a dumb question." Often we may hesitate to ask a question for fear that others might think it is dumb one. Still, we should never be reluctant to ask questions. But, it is also true, that some questions simply cannot be fully answered – at least not to the satisfaction or comprehension of human minds.

Christians sometimes encounter the latter type of questions. "How can you explain the resurrection of Jesus? How do you know what will happen when you die? How can you prove that the earth and the universe and all living things were created by a God? The human, practical, scientific mind wants understandable answers, and we cannot always give them. But that doesn't mean we are any less certain of what God, through the Bible, has told us is true. Thank God for the gift of faith and the absolute certainty of things we cannot explain.

Prayer thought: Almighty God, there are many things we cannot fully comprehend. Still, we know that if we confess that Jesus is Lord and believe in our hearts that God raised him from the dead, we will be saved. (Romans 10:9) Grant this Lord unto us all. Amen.

OLD YET NEW

By the way, does the name Goeffrey Chaucer mean anything to you? If you like English literature, you are certainly familiar. And chances are that at some point in your educational career you were introduced to Chaucer's *Canterbury Tales*. Well, Chaucer lived a long time ago and died in London all the way back in the year 1400.

The works of some authors survive for not just years or decades, but for centuries. Given the number of authors there have been through the years, remaining a prominent author for centuries is quite unusual. There's just something special about their writings. We may learn from them. We may be inspired by them, amused, or just entertained.

The Bible, of course, is the most recognized and revered of all works – not because of its prose and poetry, but because of its message. It is the message of God's plan for all of us through Jesus Christ – an eternal message that will never grow old, so long as the world exists.

Prayer thought: Lord God, may we heed the words of the Apostle Paul to Timothy – "…devote yourself to the reading of Scripture…" (I Timothy 4:13). Help us treasure your gift of Scripture. In Jesus' name. Amen.

DIRECT ORDER OR OPPORTUNITY?

By the way, do you ever get tired of hearing the word "should?" We heard it as children. "You should always wash your hands. You should study harder. You should be nicer to your brothers and sisters." And the concept is around in adulthood, too. "You should exercise more. You should save more for retirement. You should stay away from all those lovely foods that add pounds," and so forth and so on.

Even as children we knew the admonitions were correct, and we know many of them are correct now. But we didn't get good grades just because we knew we should, and we don't always take care of ourselves even though we know we should.

It isn't easy. But God would have us seek to do things that are helpful to ourselves and those around us, not simply because someone has said we should, but because we know they are pleasing to Him. And with His help, we can.

Prayer thought: When the Apostle Paul wrote to the Colossians, he encouraged them to "…walk in a manner worthy of the Lord, fully pleasing to him" (Colossians 1:10). Lead us, Heavenly Father, to do the same. In Jesus' name. Amen.

JUDGMENT OR DISCERNMENT

I need 50 copies." That's the kind of thing you might hear in an office. We copy a lot of things. Most things we buy and use are simply copies of an initial prototype. Isn't it nice that people are not simply copies? How nice it is that God did not choose to make all of his human creations exactly alike. Of course, you might say that it may not have been necessary for Him to make all of us quite as different as we are. Differences can be wonderful. Differences can also cause concern, lack of understanding, and, of course, conflict.

It's possible that all of us could use a little help from time to time in accepting those who are different. When it comes to behavior that is clearly against God's will, we should never blindly accept. But when it comes to other things – customs, dress, food preferences, language, and so forth, we should always avoid judgment that diminishes the other person. After all, they are God's creations, too.

Prayer thought: You are the great creator, of God, and you call upon us to show respect and love to those around us. Let us be slow to judge our fellow human beings, for they, too, are your creations. We pray in Jesus' name. Amen.

A New Attitude

The cell phone or iPad or computer you purchased a year ago was new at the time. And now, a short time later, it is just one of so many things that have been eclipsed by newer technology…and your "new and improved" piece of hardware is not the latest, and may even be passé.

New is not always the answer, but new can be very good. Ask yourself: Are there new opportunities in my life that I know would bring good? Is there a new attitude that can change my outlook on life? Now may be the time to make some of those new things part of your life.

God has promised to make us new, and He offers many new blessings. In His Word He promises love, joy, peace, forgiveness, contentment, eternity and many more prized possessions for those who live in faith. In faith, enjoy this new day!

Prayer thought: Almighty God, you have promised us newness. In your Word you declared that "…if anyone is in Christ, he is a new creation" (II Corinthians 5:17). We thank you that the old has passed away and that, because of Jesus Christ, we can be new. Amen.

DESTINATIONS

You may have heard the expression, "Footprints in the sands of time were not made sitting down." I guess it could also be said: "Simply having footprints in the sands of time proves very little – particularly if they just go in a never ending circle."

The point of leaving a mark on history is to leave a positive one – footprints, as it were, that lead somewhere meaningful. Too many lives, unfortunately, are filled with a lot of motion and activity, just going around in circles but never getting to a worthwhile destination.

Where is your life headed? Do you notice others along the way? Are those around you important to you? Do you believe in a final destination prepared for you and others by a loving God? It's good for all of us to occasionally stop, to look at our lives, and to ask God to help us chart a course or follow a pathway that is truly meaningful, worthwhile, and God-pleasing.

Prayer thought: Father in Heaven, you have shown us in your Word that it is always best to follow in the footsteps of our Lord Jesus Christ. Amen.

UNSEEN BEAUTY

I've been father to a number of children in my life, and each one was frustrated at one time or another with a personal problem or inability. "I just don't get it. I'm just dumb." Or "I wish my hair was not so curly. I'm ugly." Or "I'm just no good at basketball. I'm a failure." Or "Nobody likes me." And each time I heard something like that I remembered feeling the same way at many times in my life.

We all have things about ourselves we wish we could change. We're not as confident or poised or attractive or intelligent as we would like to be. But rather than dwelling on outward things, why don't we think more about what's inside. Jesus Christ intends for us to be new and confident and joyful and beautiful on the inside. He alone can make us that way. And with all of that going for us, it just doesn't matter as much that we can't change everything we would like to change.

Prayer thought: Father, the faith in Jesus Christ you have given as a free gift means that we are truly beautiful on the inside. Because of faith in your Son, we are assured of a beautiful hereafter. Lead us to celebrate what you have done for us on the inside! In Jesus' name. Amen.

SMILE!

If you pay attention at all, you know that there is a lot of advice being shared by a large number of people in our world today. Some of it is difficult to follow. Some advice should not be followed. But here's some advice that is fairly easy and good advice for all of us. "Smile! Your face does not belong only to you, because most of the time you cannot see it. It belongs, in part, to those who can see it. Try to make it as pleasant as possible for them."

One could say that a smile, or lack thereof, can tell you how a person is feeling in a number of ways: 1) Physically. If you are really hurting physically, it may be hard to smile. 2) Mentally. If you are troubled with worry and doubts and problems, it may be hard to smile. And 3) Spiritually. If you have no genuine relationship with a loving God – if you're heart is cluttered with guilt or desires only for yourself, heartfelt smiles will be difficult.

Why not share a genuine smile with those around you, today!

Prayer thought: Jesus, you said that you came so that we could "...have life and have it abundantly" (John 10:10). Let us always express to those around us the happiness you have brought us! Amen.

LISTENING SKILLS

Some of us are rather shy when it comes to talking in public, or even in a small group. That's not all bad. I recall something my father said on a number of occasions. I don't know the origin, but it went something like this: "Better to keep your mouth shut and have people think you are ignorant, than to open it and remove all doubt."

Actually, there are times when listening is simply better than talking. It may not suggest that we are "ignorant," but rather it may show our wisdom. Clearly, there is a time to speak and a time to listen.

In our faith life, listening is a wonderful thing to do – listening to God speak to us through His Holy Word, the Bible. And then, strengthened by what we have learned, we can look for just the right time to speak.

Prayer thought: As we read in the Bible, we know that there is "…a time to keep silence, and a time to speak…" (Ecclesiastes 3:7). Lord Jesus, help us know the best time for each. Amen.

HEARTACHE THERAPY

A friend who is a doctor in the medical field related a story of an experience she once had with her son and their cat. The son wanted to listen, with Mom's stethoscope, to the cat's heart. He didn't want to frighten the cat, so he gently held the cat and stroked it and ever-so-carefully placed the stethoscope on the cat's chest. "I can't hear it," he said to his Mom, "because the cat is purring so loudly."

It's wonderful for us too when things are going well in our lives and our hearts are at peace. We have a God who cares, and friends and family. But there are many in our world that are ignored, abused, and whose heartaches cry out for attention. We can help. We can let them know that they are loved. We can help them get to know our best friend, Jesus Christ. We can help heal broken hearts. We won't need a stethoscope, but let's listen and watch for those around us who can benefit from our love and attention.

Prayer thought: Along with the Psalmist, Heavenly Father, I pray "Let your steadfast love comfort me…" (Psalm 119:76), and lead me to share your love with others. Amen.

PROBLEMS WITH THE SOLUTION

I recently heard a political commentator say "If you think the problem is bad now, wait until we solve it."

That was probably an insightful comment. Sometimes the way we deal with problems only makes them worse…even though we are very well-intentioned. I don't have a solution for that. It seems to be our nature in life to do things that are not always helpful. Selfishness may contribute to the problem. Not seeing the larger picture, perhaps. And often our own misguided self-confidence.

Many times I have found it helps to stop for a moment, step back from the problem rather than reacting quickly, and spend a little time in prayer. "Lord, help me see this problem as an opportunity to do the right thing. Lord, help me see how you would have me address it. Lord, help me work to truly make things better."

Prayer thought: Lord God, I want to call upon you to be part of my efforts to solve problems. You said "…for it is God who works in you both to will and to work for his good pleasure" (Philippians 2:13). Be with me, for Jesus' sake. Amen.

THE MORNING NEWS

A listener to BY THE WAY recently sent me a little piece that I found both amusing and quite revealing. It's probably not new, but let me share it:

Dear God, so far it's been a good day – I haven't gossiped, I haven't lied, I haven't whined or even fussed. I haven't yelled and haven't cussed. But great the task that lies ahead…for now I must get out of bed.

It's true, isn't it! Each morning there are new challenges, new disappointments, and new trials along with all the old ones. There are so many temptations. So often we do and say things not pleasing to God. We fall into some of the same bad habits we exhibited yesterday and the day before. The good news is that God is there to remind us that there is a better way…and He is always there to help us make this day even better than the days that have gone before.

 Prayer thought: Almighty God, a Psalmist once wrote that "…a day in your courts is better than a thousand elsewhere…" (Psalm 84:10). The best way to spend this day is with you. Let us do so, for Jesus' sake. Amen.

YOU TURN

"**N**o U-Turn." We've all seen those signs, haven't we? And there are times when making a U-turn would be a lot easier and quicker than driving around many blocks or even miles on the interstate, in order to get going the opposite direction.

Are there times in your life, too, when you wish you could make a U-turn? There are things in the lives of all of us that we wish we could change. A U-turn would be nice. But in our lives, U-turns are even more difficult then they are on the highway.

Fortunately, there are people around us who can help. And, of course, God has promised to be there to help. He helps by reminding us through His Word of the wrong directions we have chosen. He reminds us of the sacrifice of Jesus that assures us that forgiveness is available. Then He offers strength through prayer and through the working of the Holy Spirit to turn us around. He not only allows U-turns. He encourages them.

Prayer thought: Lord God, let us always honor your admonition that we "…turn away from evil and do good…" (Psalm 34:14 and I Peter 3:11). In Jesus' name we pray. Amen.

TRUE GIFTS

The Golden Rule. It's a good one to follow. Now there's a new one. I read recently of what someone called the "Platinum" Rule: "Do onto others as they would have you do unto them." It's just a slight change in perspective, but the thought has some merit.

We've all heard of the husband who loved his wife and wanted to buy her something very nice. So he bought her a new chain saw. The thought may have been a good one. The follow through failed to really consider what she may have appreciated receiving.

We may do that with our God, as well. We may think giving financial gifts to church and attending worship with some regularity are the best gifts. But what about the gifts of our hearts and our lives – truly living our faith at all times? What about prayer? What about sharing our faith with others? Let's always seek God's will!

 Prayer thought: Lord God, give us the wisdom to know how best to serve you and those around us. In Jesus' name. Amen.

THE BLAME GAME

The Civil War in the United States started more than 150 years ago. That's a long time. One would think that by now the war would be largely forgotten. Not so.

Discussions about that war continue. Blame is still cast about. As is so often the case, we look back and find ways to place blame on people and events of the past for what may be happening today. In current political disputes it is common to hear that the blame for our problems today rests with the opposing party, the previous administration, or some other individuals or organizations.

Why is it so important to place blame? Perhaps the reason people blame others is that there is only one other choice. If it's not their fault, it must be ours. Join me in praying that our Lord Jesus Christ would lead all of us to assume responsibility for the present and future, and stop excusing our failures by blaming others.

 Prayer thought: Yes, Lord Jesus, only you can help us fully recognize those things that are not in keeping with your will for us, and only you can lead us to own up to our sins of blaming others. Lead us to do so. Amen.

TOO MUCH OF A GOOD THING?

By the way, have you followed some of the studies that have been done with those who have been recipients of large sums of money from winning the lottery? The stories are often not too encouraging. Too much money too quickly can cause all sorts of problems. Some have even said winning was the worst thing that could have happened to them. Some of us think those stories are just designed to make those of us who have never had a lot of money feel better. Many of us will claim that we could do a better job of handling the windfall.

As nice as it might be to have at least a little bit bigger bank account and a few more possessions, what Jesus once said is proven to be true over and over again in our world – these words: *"Watch out! Be on your guard against all kinds of greed; life does not consist in an abundance of possessions"* (Luke 12:15 NIV).

Possessions, too, can be gifts from God, but thank God, there is so much more to life.

Prayer thought: Loving Father, you have given us much for which to be thankful. Yet, at times, we live and work as if we need more. Forgive us our greediness and lead us to appreciate your important gifts of faith in Jesus Christ and the promise of life eternal. In Jesus' name. Amen.

DID YOU HEAR ABOUT...?

In a whisper) Come here. I have something I want to tell you.

If you really want to get someone's attention, whispering is almost always more effective than shouting. There's just something about being let in on some new information, or some new rumor, or something to be kept "secret" that intrigues us.

Some things, of course, should be kept quiet. We can always find an appropriate way to do that. But when it is gossip or a piece of information that makes others look bad, too many people find pleasure in "quietly" passing the information on to others. And those people may "quietly" pass the message on to others.

I don't know all the motivations, but you will probably agree that a lot of good seldom comes from whispering gossip. The Book of Proverbs in the Bible talks about an unfortunate result of gossip when it says *"A whisperer separates close friends"* (Proverbs 16:28). It's true. Let's avoid doing that.

Prayer thought: Lord God, our selfishness and pride can lead us to do and say things that are offensive to you and hurtful to others. For Jesus sake, rid of the temptation to gossip. Amen.

Sooner Or Later

By the way, are you a procrastinator? If you are, I'll give you a little extra time to respond…(Ready?) My wife, has at times, accused me of being a procrastinator. And *some* day I am going to show her that she is wrong.

Many of us do put things off. Sometimes it's just a fairly simple task. We might even think about it with some regularity, but we just never take the time to accomplish it.

It's true, if you want to make an easy job a difficult one, just keep putting it off. If you've been thinking about reaching out to someone in need, or spending a bit more time in prayer or reading God's Word, or volunteering at church, or getting a little more exercise, or losing some weight, or whatever – if you know it is a good and God-pleasing thing to do, don't put it off. Don't procrastinate. Some great things can result – and they will result sooner, rather than later.

Prayer thought: Lord, you have given to each of us only a limited amount of time on this earth. Move us to use it wisely, doing those things that are truly important now, rather than delaying. In Jesus' name. Amen.

PRODUCING GOOD FRUIT

The idea of good works is something that has always been part of discussions in the Christian church and in other contexts, as well. How do we motivate people toward good works? Do people do good things simply for some kind of reward? Lots of questions and opinions.

A Scripture passage in the New Testament helps. It calls upon Christians to be *"fruitful in every good work..."* (Colossians 1:10). Andrew Murray, a Christian pastor in the late 1800s and early 1900s put it this way: "A machine can do work; only life can bear fruit." If work is done simply because it is compelled, or done out of obligation or fear, it may bring about good, but God's definition of a good work is more than that. Just as you do not have to force a tree to bring forth fruit, so you never have to force good works. They are the natural result of faith.

I pray your life of faith rather automatically produces good fruit.

Prayer thought: Oh God, you have given to me the powerful gift of faith in Jesus Christ. I pray that this great gift will always lead me to do those things that manifest my faith, for it is in Jesus' name I pray. Amen.

LIFE GUIDANCE

Have you ever driven in heavy fog…or in a blinding rain or snow storm? "White knuckle rides" we call them. It's not easy to see where you are going, and it's a bit intimidating. Often times when I have found myself in that situation I have been passed by drivers who, obviously, were not as concerned as I was. In fact, I worried a bit for those drivers and prayed they would not experience a serious accident.

In life, too, there are those who charge ahead into the fog, not knowing or caring what lies ahead. Many suffer tragic consequences. If you can't see very clearly what lies ahead in your life, let me suggest that you slow down. Take a few moments to consider the risks that may lie ahead. Look to Jesus Christ, the light of the world, for some direction and protection. He does see what lies ahead for you, and He is there to provide life-saving and soul-saving guidance.

Prayer thought: I praise you, Almighty God in Jesus name, "For you are my rock and my fortress; and for your name's sake you lead me and guide me" (Psalm 31:3). Amen.

TAKE IT IN STRIDE

If you've ever watched a little league baseball game or some other event where children compete, you know how differently children react in certain situations. Some children seem devastated by a personal "goof" in the game. Some don't seem to mind at all. Some can't handle defeat. Some take it in stride.

I remember a little league game in which one of my young sons played. Already in the first inning, the opposing team was up by eleven runs. I thought my son might be getting discouraged so I managed to whisper to him, "Don't feel bad." And he replied, "Why should I, Dad? We haven't been up to bat yet."

I guess we could look into any office or store or factory or school or home and discover similar differences in the way people deal with victories and defeats. A competitive spirit and personal pride can be good, but they should not become obsessions that ruin our ability to enjoy life.

Prayer thought: Lord God, help us to keep things in perspective so that we do not become arrogant in victory or despondent in defeat. Help us always to show love and concern for others. In Jesus' name. Amen.

Don't Grow Weary

There are times in the lives of all of us when "doing the right thing" is just not as easy as it sounds. It may be difficult to do what God would have you do. It may be difficult to avoid doing things that would not be pleasing to God. There may be repercussions. You may end up on the wrong side of those who are more powerful than you are.

When you live with honesty as a normal trait; when you reach out to, and stand up for, the needy, the misunderstood, and the falsely accused; when you choose not to follow the latest questionable fad, even if it is "politically correct," you may never be applauded.

Just remember that God sees and appreciates what you do in following Him. Those who benefit from your efforts will be thankful, too, even if they never have a chance to thank you. Whatever you do, don't grow weary of well doing!

Prayer thought: Heavenly Father, help us to heed the words of the Apostle Paul: "Therefore take up the whole armor of God, that you may be able to withstand the evil day…to stand firm" (Ephesians 6:13). In Jesus' name. Amen.

ON PURPOSE

We live in an age of self-gratification. There are so many things in our world tempting us to "do this...buy that...go here...experience this." And if the experience is not quite what we had hoped for, we're ready to try something else. But so many things are just dead-end roads.

Helen Keller once said, "Many persons have a wrong idea about what constitutes true happiness. It is not attained through self-gratifications, but through fidelity to a worthy purpose."

It's probably good for all of us occasionally to look at the purposes to which we have devoted ourselves. Are they worthy? Are they God-pleasing? Are they bringing some real happiness? If not, look for some new ones. Who knows what happiness may await.

Prayer thought: Heavenly Father, with the strength and resolve you supply, lead us to be faithful to the wonderful purpose of living as redeemed brothers and sisters of Jesus Christ! In his name. Amen.

Small Vs. Significant

By the way, what are some of the things that really get you upset? Someone has wisely said: "You can tell the size of a person by the size of the things that upset that person." If you think about that in your life, you might find that there are times when small things really do get to you.

There are things in our world that truly justify being upset. The immoral and questionable character of so much of what is on TV; the prevalence of child abuse and spouse abuse; the popularity of using violent measures to accomplish political and so-called religious goals; the plight of the impoverished; the sick and hungry and orphaned around the world; and so many more things that are so much more important than long lines at the fast food restaurant.

We would all be grateful if the "small" annoyances would go away, but it would be well for us to spend our energy praying for and working for some of the "bigger" things.

 Prayer thought: Heavenly Father, lead me to be "big" in matters that are really important – those things that truly make a difference for good. In Jesus' name. Amen.

YES OR NO

A simple question deserves a simple answer. Often, however, that's not the way it works. "Do you have homework," I asked my daughter. The response was "Not much."

Later I asked, "Did you finish your homework?" And the response was "Almost." "So how much do you have to do?" And she replied, "Just a minute, I'm on the phone."

I guess we're all good at failing to give direct answers to direct questions. A simple "yes" or "no" would often suffice. We all may "beat around the bush" occasionally, but it's nice to know the Lord has chosen not to do so. When we ask for forgiveness, He says "Yes." When we ask about what happens when we die, He says "I have a place for you." When we ask about how we relate to others, He says "Love one another." His Word, the Bible, is full of words that assure us of His love and provide valuable answers.

Prayer thought: Almighty God, we are grateful that we can always count on all that you have said and all that you have clearly promised. As we are told in your Holy Word, "All the promises of God find their Yes in him" (Jesus Christ) (II Corinthians 1:20). In his name. Amen.

BACK TO BASICS

If you are tuned in to just about any type of sporting activity, you will frequently hear coaches and others talk about "fundamentals." We are told athletes seldom succeed without hard work, discipline, and attention to fundamentals. Of course, it's true in many areas of life.

One of the legendary stories of the late football coach Vince Lombardi is a story related to fundamentals. After losing what should have been a victory for the Green Bay Packers, their coach, Mr. Lombardi addressed his team. While pointing to the football he was holding in his hand, he is to have said: "It's time to get back to the basics. Gentlemen, this is a football."

So what are the fundamentals in your life? One of them should be your recognition of your God. You are here solely because of God's grace. Your life is a gift. Faith in Jesus Christ is a gift. The promise of life everlasting is a gift, a secure promise for all those with faith in Christ. Trusting in God is a fundamental – a basic we should never be without.

Prayer thought: Lord Jesus, you are the "founder and perfecter of our faith" (Hebrews 12:2). Give us always the solid faith to know that you are the fundamental link to our Heavenly Father and to life everlasting. Amen.

Fewer Big Problems

I'm sure you have had the experience of something quite small causing a problem. It may have been a small part that kept your automobile from running properly…or a simple connection that kept your computer from working …or forgetting one key ingredient in a cooking recipe that resulted in a not-too-tasty dish. Oh, we worry about terrorism and the economy and the price of health insurance, but often it's the little things done by family members or neighbors or coworkers, or the little annoyances in life that really frustrate us. At times, they grow into BIG problems for us.

We contribute to the BIG problems, too, don't we? The small lies, the small indiscretions, the small disagreements, the small bad choices can easily grow into BIG problems. It is good for all of us to keep an eye on the small temptations that lead us astray. If we do that, and seek to do those things pleasing to God in all areas of our lives, we may face many fewer BIG problems.

Prayer thought: At times, Lord Jesus, the sins we commit seem small to us. We overlook them. We ignore them… until they become big problems. You are offended by all sin, but please keep us on the lookout for small sins that can become so destructive. In your holy name. Amen.

MOVING VIOLATIONS

I'm sure you've had an experience similar to this one. You're traveling down the interstate. The speed limit is 65. Traffic is moving at a speed somewhere between 70 and 75, some going even faster. You approach the top of a small hill and notice a lot of brake lights in front of you. Drivers in front of you have spotted a state trooper with radar parked in the median ahead.

It's a pretty good picture of how we human beings act. We know what is right – the correct things to do, but we fudge a bit. And then, when faced with the prospect of being called to account or being penalized for our actions, we hit the brakes.

Some violations, of course, are more serious than others. But in all the things in life, God would have us follow what He has said is pleasing to Him. In so doing, we can avoid slamming on the brakes.

Prayer thought: Oh God, we continue to give into temptation and later regret our actions. Let us look to you as we determine how we will act so that we can avoid doing what is not according to your will. In Jesus' name. Amen.

FULL CIRCLE OF KINDNESS

Kindness," it's been said, "is a hard thing to give away…because it usually comes back."

It's true, isn't it! Kindness is like a boomerang. You give it away, but it usually comes back. Often when you're kind to someone, they return your kindness with their own

It's often seen quite dramatically in little things. For example, a smile is contagious. A genuine compliment often results is some kindness sent back. Try hugging or praising a child and see what a difference it makes in their outlook on life. Take time to listen to someone and see how much they appreciate it. Open a door for someone. Let someone with only one or two items to purchase go ahead of you in the checkout line. Yield to another driver at an intersection.

No one has been kinder to us than our loving God. And there's no better way to respond to that kindness than by passing God's love and kindness on to others.

Prayer thought: In your holy Word, loving God, you directed us to "Put on then, as God's chosen ones… kindness" (Colossians 3:12). What a wonderful way for us to show your love in Jesus Christ to others. Amen

THE POWER TOOL OF FAITH

Some of us men have a real appreciation for tools. I've never met a power tool I didn't like. And there are many tools in the garage that haven't been used in years, even though there may be projects around the house calling out for them.

All of us have many "tools" in life, as it were, too. We have the wherewithal – the knowledge, resources and abilities – to get things done, but for whatever reason, the tools are off in some corner of our lives gathering dust.

Christians have received the gift of faith, and that gift is intended to accomplish great things. But maybe that gift ends up, unfortunately, in the basement of one's life.

No matter how distant your faith may be today, it still has the potential for real power. Ask God to help move it more to the center of your life, and then watch for some wonderful things to happen.

 Prayer thought: Lord Jesus, the gift of faith in you is not intended to be ignored. Rather, it is to be alive. It is intended to be at the center of my life and to be used for your purposes. Give me a living and lively faith. Amen.

PRAY ALWAYS

I've always believed that prayer is something that doesn't need to be very formal. There are so many times in a day when a short, two word prayer is appropriate: "Thanks, Lord!" And at other times it may be a simple "Lord, I need some help with this," or "Lord Jesus Christ, help me understand what is going on," or "Lord, please help and comfort those people who are suffering," or "Lord, I'm sorry."

But there is the occasion when devoting a little quiet time to prayer is very good. Prayer is more than just a list of requests. It is listening, as well. Maybe it is quietly recalling a favorite Scripture passage or a favorite hymn stanza. Think of that passage from the Bible where God says *"Be still and know that I am God"* (Psalm 46:10). Brief conversations with God are always appropriate. So are those when we are "still," patiently having an uninterrupted conversation with a God who is never too busy to listen and to care.

Prayer thought: The Prophet Isaiah spoke words true for us, as well. "…the effect of righteousness will be peace, and the result of righteousness, quietness and trust forever" (Isaiah 32:17). May these words be true for us. In Jesus' name. Amen.

REALLY LIVING

Two questions for you today. Here's the first: What do we really need to live? And here's the second, which will sound very similar: What do we need to really live?

What do we really need to live? We could mention the three things commonly mentioned: food, clothing, and shelter. These are essential.

And what do we need to really live? Now that's a different question. In his sermon on the mount, Jesus asked: *"Is not life more that food, and the body more than clothing?"* (Matthew 6:25). Of course life is more than the bare essentials. If you want to *really* live you need love, joy, peace of mind, acceptance, forgiveness, and a whole host of other things that God offers freely. In fact, without the things that God can give through faith in Jesus Christ, it's impossible to *really* live. I pray that you are *really* living!

Prayer thought: Lord Jesus, you intended for us to really live – to know and experience all the special blessings you shower upon those with faith in you. Fill our hearts with thankfulness, lead us to look to you so that we can really live. Amen.

SECTION II

COMMITMENT TO GOD AND THANKFULNESS

BY THE WAY

THOUGHTS FOR YOUR DAY

To God The Glory

I t is generally acknowledged that the greatest composer of all time is Johann Sebastian Bach. A contemporary of his – Georg Frideric Handel – was a great composer, too. He is best known for his oratorio MESSIAH that included words from the King James Bible and music from his inspired mind

Like Bach, Handel was successful and applauded during his lifetime, but chose to give credit to God. Like Bach, the pieces he composed all carried an inscription from his hand that was simply "Soli Deo Gloria," which means "to God alone the glory." The compositions were popular and have been extremely well received since they were composed. Still, both composers chose to give the glory to the God who was honored by their music. How nice it would be if an inscription on those things we are able to accomplish could likewise be "Soli Deo Gloria!"

Prayer thought: Almighty and Glorious God, you deserve all the glory. What we are able to do in your Kingdom is due to your grace and mercy in Jesus Christ. We praise you and consider it a privilege to give you all the glory. In Jesus' name. Amen.

The Most Valuable Gift

I love you. I love you today and everyday. I want the best for you. Look around you. So much beauty. So many special people in your life. There's acceptance and forgiveness. There's hope and joy and comfort. When you're facing trials and when you fail, I love you. When you are filled with doubt and despair, I'm there. When you are sad and alone, I am with you. Through all the ups and downs of your life, I love you. I demonstrated that love for you most dramatically with the gift of my Son, Jesus Christ. He was the most valuable gift I could have given. He brought you real life and real faith. He showed you my love, and now you can share that love with others.

Well, He didn't say so in exactly those words. But that is the beautiful message of a loving Heavenly Father. He does love you! Count on it!

Prayer thought: Thanks, Lord Jesus, for expressing your love to us in so many ways. We need your love and we need to be reminded of it. Now, give us hearts full of thanksgiving for it. In your name. Amen.

HOW GREAT!

It's clearly one of the most spectacular sights. To see it, you have to get away from the city lights on a clear night without the brightness of a full moon. Looking up, you can see a remarkable display – the brilliant canopy of stars. I remember being so impressed as a child seeing all the stars. I still am.

Among other things, the experience is a reminder of how small we human being are in the vast expanse of the universe. Yet, despite our smallness, we remain the most significant of all of God's marvelous creations. Imagine that. The God who put the stars in the sky really cares for the likes of you and me.

I'm grateful. And taking the time to occasionally step into what some call the Cathedral of Creation to view God's handiwork is a great way to say "Thanks, Lord, how great thou art!"

Prayer thought: Along with the Psalmist we testify: "The heavens declare the glory of God, and the sky above proclaims his handiwork" (Psalm 19:1). O God, how marvelous is your creation…and your love for us! Amen.

It's a Song Worth Singing

Christians are very familiar with the words from the Psalm, *"Oh sing to the Lord a new song"* (Psalm 98:1). Dietrich Bonhoeffer, who was martyred for his faith in Jesus Christ, once wrote a little piece about the "new song." He describes it as something familiar to Christians as they greet the morning with thanks to God for a new day. It is the song the morning stars sang together at the creation of the world. (Job 38:7) It is the song the Children of Israel sang after passing safely through the Red Sea, it is the Magnificat of Mary, the song of Paul and Silas when imprisoned.

Bonhoeffer mentioned just a few. There are so many… and their crescendos grow whenever Christians remember the eternal blessings that come from a loving God. There are too many to even remember, but they are all worth a song. Sing your song today. Sing it to the Lord!

 Prayer thought: Loving Lord Jesus, make this our prayer – "I will sing of the steadfast love of the Lord (you), forever" (Psalm 89:1). In your name we pray. Amen.

Children – Precious Gifts

My wife and I have sometimes talked about how difficult it would be at this point in our lives to have young children. We remember crying children, toys all over the place, loads of laundry, getting up during the night, and handprints on the walls. While we may not wish to go back to those days, there are times we think back and realize those days were some of the very happiest we have experienced.

Children are challenging. If you have young ones, I know what you are going through. But appreciate the gifts God has given you, as tough as the task may be…because sometimes we don't appreciate what we have until much later. When it comes to children, the miracle of their laughter, wonder, and love of life is something all of us should appreciate, even with the handprints. They are, indeed, precious gifts from God.

 Prayer thought: Indeed, "…children are a heritage from the Lord…" (Psalm 127:3). You have given us the precious gifts of children in our world, Lord God. May we always appreciate them and point them to you, for Jesus' sake. Amen.

DEEP-ROOTED TRUST

Trust. It is such an important thing, but not always easy to find. In the Old Testament of the Bible is this beautiful passage that speaks to trust:

Blessed is the man who trusts in the Lord... He is like a tree planted by water that sends out its roots by the stream and does not fear when heat comes for its leaves remain green, and is not anxious in the year of drought, for it does not cease to bear fruit.

(Jeremiah 7:7-8)

We could all pray for more of that "trust," couldn't we! We depend too much upon ourselves. We worry about the future. We fear the many crazy things happening in our world – and there are many of them. It may at times seem to be an oversimplification, but it's true: As with a tree, if your roots are deep and strong, (trusting in the Lord) you needn't worry as much about the drought or the wind!

Prayer thought: By myself, Heavenly Father, I could never withstand the things that threaten. Your blessings in Jesus Christ sustain me. Give me, always, a deeply-rooted trust in you. In Jesus' name. Amen.

THANKS FOR LIVING

I have a friend who went through a rare and serious operation several years ago. By God's grace, he is doing well and is very hopeful about the future. He told me his wife occasionally looks at him or puts her arm around him and says quietly, "Thanks for living." He then jokingly says "the bar has been set pretty low for me. All that is expected of me is to live."

I like the approach of his wife – "thanks for living." Too often we have a whole list of expectations and demands for spouses, children, and others around us – so much so that we may never stop and simply thank God for the life that He has given to them and to us. Every human being is a gift of life! So, "thanks, Lord, for giving me life, and thanks for the life you have given to those around me."

Prayer thought: Lord God, how often I take for granted the lives of friends and loved ones and fail to fully appreciate those you have brought into my life. Bless them. Protect them. Help me to show my love for them. In Jesus' name. Amen.

MORE THAN I DESERVE

In his book, *The Great Divorce*, C.S. Lewis tells how disgusted a citizen of hell becomes when he discovers that one of heaven's citizens had been a murderer on earth. The lost one – the citizen of hell - claims it is not fair. The lost one takes a stand and demands "his rights." To that, the citizen of heaven – the saved murderer – says: "I didn't get my rights, thank God, or I wouldn't be here. I got something far better."

The "far better" thing, of course, was forgiveness – won for the murderer and for all people by the sacrifice of Jesus Christ – His death as payment for the sins of all people. Faith in Jesus Christ brings that "far better" thing to us. If we claimed simply "our rights," there would be no hope. We would surely be doomed. But thank God, He had something "far better" in mind.

Prayer thought: Almighty God, we know from your Word that if the Son sets us free, we will be free indeed. (John 8:36) How grateful we are that your Son, Jesus Christ, paid the price for our sins so that we will not be eternally doomed. Amen.

COINCIDENCE? PROBABLY NOT

Coincidence. Coincidence is defined in one dictionary as "something that happens by chance in a surprising or remarkable way."

Have you had coincidence experiences? No doubt you have. It is quite likely that at times in your life you have said something such as "What a coincidence." It just sort of happened, we think. When the coincidence brings a special blessing, you may truly be grateful for that the coincidence came along at just the right time.

The dictionary definition is generally accurate. There is, however, one small change that would make that definition considerably more accurate. Here is that definition: Coincidence is "something that happens by God's design (not by chance) in a surprising or remarkable way." So many things we can't explain are simply God working in our lives. It could be said that "a coincidence is a small miracle where God prefers to remain anonymous."

Prayer thought: Almighty God, we praise and thank you for being in our lives in miraculous ways, even though we so often fail to see your hand. For Jesus' sake, lead us to be mindful of your goodness. Amen.

BALANCE

Some years ago a friend of mine gave me a little card with one word on it. The word was "BALANCE." It sat on my desk for a long time. It was a good reminder of something quite helpful in life.

In good times we may see life as a pleasant journey. At other times we may feel as if it is anything but a pleasant journey. But life, where it is lived day in and day out, is normally somewhere in between.

To expect never ending mountain top experiences will only lead to disappointment. Giving in to despair is giving up. "Balance" is the ability to keep things in perspective. Both the highs and the lows are fleeting. No matter where we are in the journey of life, the Lord Jesus Christ travels with us – there for us on the good days, the bad days, and everything in between.

Prayer thought: Loving Father, we know you have been with us throughout our lives. We know you will be our God in all the days ahead. Remind us that you are with us now, today, this very moment, for Jesus' sake. Amen.

ONE OF A KIND

By the way, you are SPECIAL. That's true, but you might respond by saying "that's just a worn out, trite statement intended to make me feel good. But I don't feel very 'special.'"

It was back in 1953 that scientists identified deoxyribonucleic acid, commonly known as DNA. That discovery has lead to many advances and other discoveries since that time. One thing DNA has shown conclusively is that each of us is unique – a special creation. It's fairly obvious that everyone is different without DNA evidence, but DNA is a scientific explanation of what God has done from the beginning. He is the Creator, and He chose to make each of His creations one-of-a-kind.

Think of that. God made you, and then threw away that mold. And He loves you. And He loves each and every one of His creations. Today, thank God for how special He made you to be.

 Prayer thought: Lord God, "I praise you, for I am fearfully and wonderfully made" (Psalm 139:14). You have made me one of a kind. I am your "special" child. For Jesus' sake, make my love for you special. Amen.

THE LORD BE WITH YOU

One of the things Christian pastors say to their people – in worship services and in other settings – is "The Lord be with you." And the people respond by saying "And also with you."

The exchange is not so much a prayer asking that the Lord would be kind enough to be with us, but rather a statement of fact that the Lord, indeed, is with us. No matter what happens in our lives, Jesus Christ is there.

So the phrase "The Lord be with you" is an invitation to remember that the Lord is with us – to know beyond a shadow of a doubt that there is no place we can go and nothing we can do that will take us away from the watchful eye of a loving Lord. And knowing that can make our days and our deeds so much brighter. Wherever you are today and whatever you are doing, the Lord be with you!

Prayer thought: Lord Jesus, how blessed we are that you are always with us. What a great love and concern that demonstrates. We thank you and pray we might always feel and appreciate your presence. Amen.

GOOD MEDICINE

Those who study such things tell us that laughter is actually very healthy. It has a positive effect on your physical wellbeing. Given the condition of our world, many of us might claim that there are just too few things that make us want to laugh. But maybe we're not looking carefully enough.

Have you watched a young child giggle over a new toy? Have you listened to teenagers laughing about what older folks might consider the silliest things? Do you remember some of the great humorists who made us laugh without being crude and vulgar? Are you open to laughing at yourself for the humorous things you sometimes do?

Well, I pray you'll find a reason to laugh today – not only because it is good for you, but because, as the great reformer Martin Luther once said, "It is pleasing to God whenever you rejoice or laugh from the bottom of your heart."

Prayer thought: Dear God, in the midst of life you give us reasons and occasions that warm our hearts and touch them with happiness. We praise you for giving us times to enjoy laughter. Amen.

THANKS FOR THE MEMORIES

Each of us has experienced the loss of something important to us. As a child, it may have been the loss of a favorite toy or being separated from a childhood friend. Most of us, at one time or another, have lost something valuable – a job, a prized possession, our health that once was better than it is today.

One of the most helpful pieces of advice I have heard when it comes to such things is "Don't cry because it is over. Smile because it happened." While I may be inclined to complain because something has come to an end, I seldom look back to say "Praise the Lord that it happened. Praise the Lord I had a chance to experience that. Praise the Lord because that special person was part of my life. Praise the Lord that once I was able to do all those things."

Smile, because God has done so many great things in your life!

Prayer thought: There's no way, O God, that we could recall all the wonderful things we have experienced in life. Still, help us to be grateful that we were blessed in so many ways. Help us to smile in remembrance. In Jesus' name. Amen.

A CERTAIN DESTINATION

If you travel from time to time, you may have had an experience similar to one I've had. You wake up in the morning and it takes you a brief moment to remember exactly where you are. I woke up recently from a nap on an airplane and couldn't immediately remember where I was headed.

Sometimes life is a bit like that. We lose track of where we are headed, or we haven't given much thought to where we are going.

Do you have a destination in mind? Not just for today or for this week, but where are you headed ultimately? Does this journey of your life have a place to ultimately "land?"

If you are a Christian, you can answer with all clarity, "YES." God has prepared a place for me. I know where I am going…and I know my God is with me always, wherever I go, until I get there.

Prayer thought: Dear Jesus, how fortunate I am that I have a destination you have prepared for me. I'm not certain when I will arrive, but I am certain I will arrive because of your gift to me of salvation. I praise and thank you. Amen.

FOREVER FAITH

One of the first words a child learns to say as he or she clutches a toy or a favorite blanket or a piece of candy is "MINE!" We may not be quite as vocal about it as we grow in years, but there remains this strong sense that some things are OURS – we own them.

Still, if we are honest about it, we have to admit that all our good and worthwhile possessions are gifts from God. The greatest gift He gave to many of us is the gift of faith in Jesus Christ. And it may be one of a very small number of things that we can claim truly are ours. It is my faith. God gave it to me. It is a highly prized possession. I pray no one ever takes it from me…for it is the one possession that I will be able to carry with me forever. Thanks, Lord, for your gift to me of faith in Jesus Christ!

Prayer thought: Lord Jesus, give me your strength, grace, and inspiration to hold firmly to my faith in you. It is a priceless possession. It is a treasure more valuable than any other. In your name I pray. Amen.

HE IS ABLE

For a number of years, a good friend of mine who is a CPA has helped me with my taxes. There was a time I filled out all the forms and did all the calculations myself. But it's nice to have someone who is a professional do all of that. So much of it just seems beyond my ability to fully comprehend.

There's an old saying that "ignorance is bliss." In a sense that may be true when it comes to the things I don't understand. I don't have to worry a lot about them because I can't understand them and probably couldn't do them correctly if I had to.

In a much grander sense, I'm grateful that I don't have to worry about eternity or find a way on my own to experience it. I have a loving God who is the expert. Faith in Jesus Christ will place me in the eternal presence of that expert. What a wonderful feeling!

Prayer thought: Dear Father in heaven, your plan for me included all eternity. Through your son, Jesus Christ, the plan was sealed. To you be the praise for doing for me what I could never do for myself. In Jesus' name. Amen.

FOLLOW THE LEADER

I was on a two-lane road recently. A winding road. I was driving the speed limit, or there-abouts, and I noticed the number of cars in my rearview mirror steadily increasing. "Well," I thought, "this is one way to be a leader." But the people behind me were probably not thinking too highly of my leadership. They were anxious to have the freedom to pass me by and be their own leaders.

I suspect some in our world consider themselves leaders because so many people have no choice but to follow them. And the followers may be no happier following these leaders than the people in the cars behind me on the winding road.

Jesus provided a good example. He never forced people to follow. But many people did. Many people still do, knowing that no person or organization or government or leader can compare. Lead on, Lord. I will happily follow.

Prayer thought: Lord Jesus, of you it is said, "God exalted him at his right hand as Leader and Savior…" (Acts 5:31). Lead me, Lord, so that I might come to know better the joys along the way. In your name. Amen.

NO WAY TO LOSE

The Christian Chaplain in a nursing home was a always happy to talk about his experiences. Among other things, he talked about how wonderful it was to work with people of faith. "Those with a strong faith in Jesus Christ," he said, "look at life differently. As they battle some serious physical problems or wonder how many more days the Lord will give them on this earth, they tend to know this with great confidence – that if they die, they will be with the Lord. And, as long as they live, the Lord will be with them. Either way, the two will always be together."

It's good for all of us to pray for that kind of strong faith – the one that sees God's blessings no matter what. What a difference it can make in our lives if we know with certainty and remember regularly, that we always remain in God's loving hands!

Prayer thought: Eternal God, you have given me something that allows me to find comfort and hope in all situations – the assurance that through faith in Jesus Christ, I am never outside your loving care. Sincere thanks, in Jesus' name. Amen.

PRAISE GOD CONTINUALLY?

There's a passage in the Bible that says we should *"offer up continually…praise to God…"* (Hebrews 13:15). A young boy in Sunday School heard those words from the Bible and his response was something like this: "My bike just got a flat tire. My best friend moved away. I got a bad grade on my history test. I don't think I'll make the baseball team, and I just put a hole in my new tennis shoes. And you're telling me I'm supposed to praise God?"

I'm sure we can all identify with that response. Praising God "continually" just seems unrealistic. But what we are being encouraged to do is to remember that our God is with us in every situation. He is more powerful than any thing or any one. Whatever we are facing, we are not alone. He is there…continually. His promises are sure…continually. And we can praise Him…continually!

 Prayer thought: So many things, Lord God, distract and disturb us. It's difficult to remember your gracious kindness. No matter where we are or what we are experiencing, show us how to praise you, for Jesus' sake. Amen.

TIME LIKE A RIVER

Henry David Thoreau, known as a great nature-lover, once wrote "Time is but the stream I go a-fishing in." I'm not much of a fisherman, but I have stood on the banks of streams and rivers and know that the waters passing by are always changing and quickly gone as they head down stream. I can look up stream but I cannot see where the stream begins. I can look down stream but cannot see where the stream ends.

The river I gaze upon has flowed for thousands of years and will continue to flow in the future. My time on earth is very short, by comparison. But, of course, God has promised that time for us will not end. Those with faith in Jesus Christ will live on. None of us knows how much time we will have on earth, but we can all be grateful for the time God gives us and we can pray He will help us use time wisely.

Prayer thought: In your Holy Word, Lord God, you said "Look carefully then how you walk, not as unwise but as wise, making the best use of time…" (Ephesians 5:15, 16). Inspire us to do that for Jesus' sake. Amen.

TREASURED FRIENDS

Through the years, I have corresponded with quite a number of people I have never met. There are probably people in your experience, too, that you have never met, but something has connected you – even long distance – and you consider those persons friends.

Friends – the ones we know and see regularly – are blessings. So are those we may not have met. God has blessed us with the people He has brought into our lives. They make life so much more interesting and enjoyable. We look forward to connecting with more friends.

There's a short verse I like that speaks to the value of friendships:

> There's happiness in little things,
> There's joy in passing pleasure
> But friendships are, from year to year
> The best of all life's treasure.

Thank God for the valuable friends in your life. They are "treasures."

 Prayer thought: Dear Father, you have brought people into our lives who have been special treasures. We thank you for them and pray that you would lead us to be treasured friends to them, for Jesus' sake. Amen.

TAKE MY HAND

If you are a parent, how many times have you said to your child or children, "hold my hand?" In many situations, it is so important that they do so. But children, of course, are not always convinced. They may wish to be independent, to go it alone without help from a parent or another adult. But how wonderful it is when a child says, "Mommy…Daddy, hold my hand."

Through all of life, our loving God stands beside us and offers His hand to hold us, to lead us, to protect us. He never forces us to take His hand, but waits and longs for the time when we will say, "Lord, hold my hand." We will often choose to go it alone, but it is so much better to recognize our need for God's help. It is much better if we resolve to take advantage of the strong, leading, uplifting, and loving hand of God.

Prayer thought: Eternal Father, I need you loving, guiding, and protecting hand. I can't make it on my own. Hold me close to you. Lead me in ways you would have me go, for Jesus' sake. Amen.

HERE AND HEREAFTER

The story is told of the senior citizen who was asked by a pastor: "Do you believe in the hereafter?" To which the senior replied: "Absolutely. Several times a day I find myself somewhere asking myself, 'what am I here after.'"

There is, of course, a serious and far-reaching question about the "hereafter" – the heaven that God promised for all who believe in Jesus Christ. Some dismiss the whole notion of a heaven. But then it might be appropriate to ask "If there is no hereafter, what are we here…after? To experience life and face death? To fight for a moment in the sun? To achieve, some status, have some accomplishments?" Fortunately, Christians know that what we do here is simply a prologue to what we will experience when life here ends, and a glorious eternity begins. There is a "hereafter," and it helps inform how we live…here.

Prayer thought: Lord Jesus, because of you we are destined for the place where you are enthroned. We praise you for preparing it for us and giving us the assurance that we will share it with you. Amen.

NO SEPARATION

In the previous message I mentioned how nice it is for Christians to know that what they experience on earth is not all there is – that a heaven awaits them. Depending upon what kind of day you are having, you may be wishing you could have a little taste of heaven now. It's hard to escape the trials of life. But so long as we live on this earth, it is a great comfort to know that the Lord Jesus Christ, who awaits us in the heavenly realms, is very much with us in the here and now. This is one of my favorite Scripture passages:

> *For I am persuaded, that neither death nor life, nor angels, nor principalities, nor powers, nor things present, nor things to come, nor height, nor depth, nor any other creature, shall be able to separate us from the love of God, which is in Christ Jesus our Lord.*

(Romans 8:38, 39 KJV)

 Prayer thought: O God, your love in Jesus Christ brought us together and keeps us together. How blessed we are that nothing we encounter in this world can separate us from that love! Amen.

BUILT FOR HIM

If you've ever visited Europe and spent any time in the country of France, you may have been blessed to see some of France's great cathedrals – Notre Dame, Sacré Coeur and others. For me, the most impressive of all of them is Chartres. This cathedral, located on a higher elevation in a relatively unpopulated area, was consecrated back in 1260. It features high Gothic architecture and stunning blue stained glass – so stunning and unique that this shade of blue has come to be known as Chartres blue.

The cathedral stands today – still beautiful and impressive – as a testimony to the commitment and artistry of Christians who believed that building something of surpassing strength and elegance was a fit thing to do. After all, it was built to honor the Lord Jesus Christ, who gave everything He had for us, deserving all glory, honor, and praise.

Prayer thought: Nothing human beings build can ever testify fully to the honor and glory you deserve, Lord Jesus. Still, we remember with gratitude those who have sought in many ways to bring glory to your name. Amen.

ON LOAN

A desk I frequently use as I put some thoughts on paper for these BY THE WAY messages allows me to see, just beyond the computer screen and through a large window, a beautiful maple tree. Its appearance, of course, changes from season to season. Green leaves in the summer. Red and gold leaves in the fall. No leaves in the winter.

"To whom does this tree belong?" it could be asked. Property owners, of course, would say "it is our tree." And legally, that may be true. But no human being could begin to create from scratch a maple or anything like it.

You made it, Lord. You own it. It is yours. Like so many things, you let us "have" it and enjoy it. Too seldom do we thank you. More often we complain about raking the leaves. Forgive us, Lord, for not recognizing more often your many wonderful blessings.

 Prayer thought: "Worthy are you, our Lord and God, to receive glory and honor and power, for you created all things" (Revelation 4:11). We thank you for allowing us to enjoy what you have created. In Jesus' name. Amen.

SOMETHING TO THINK ABOUT

There's some wonderful advice in the Bible. A favorite passage of mine is this:

…whatever is true…honorable…just…pure… lovely, whatever is commendable – if there is any excellence, if there is anything worthy of praise – think about these things.

(Philippians 4:8)

"Well," you might respond, "that sounds nice but what about all the devastating wars and conflicts in the world? What about the threat of terrorism and nuclear weapons? What about drug usage? What about struggles people face in finding some financial security? What about the breakdown of the family?" We'd love to think about some good things, but there just seem to be too many bad things.

Well, God still encourages us to think of the good. He reminds us of what Jesus Christ has accomplished for us. Step away just long enough today from the bad news to look for the many wonderful blessings God continues to provide. That could provide some very nice relief!

Prayer thought: Dear Father, the world around us invests so much time and effort in thinking about and promoting what is evil. Keep evil from our minds and fill them with thoughts pleasing to you. In Jesus' name. Amen.

GOD OF CREATION

Isabel was the first hurricane I personally experienced in my lifetime. Being on the east coast at the time, I watched the storm. For several hours during the worst of it, I found a place outside that I believed to be safe and witnessed, first hand, the passing power of this natural phenomenon.

Among other things, I watched the trees – some of them very tall and quite wide. Twisting and turning and reluctantly giving up some of their leaves and small branches, they stood tall and strong and survived the winds and rain. "Whoever designed those trees," I thought, "had to be a genius." Sure, some trees came down in the storm, but hundreds of thousands of others withstood the test.

Of course, I know who designed the tree…and all the other wonderful things in nature. There's only One who could – the loving God of all creation. What a marvelous job He did!

 Prayer thought: Some day, Almighty God, we may know more clearly your amazing power to create. For now, we just stand in awe, marvel at what you have done, and thank you for the incredible creation that surrounds us. Amen.

Pray For Our Country

Among the many things that amaze me in recurring political campaigns is the myriad of "easy answers" to complex problems. Many candidates claim they have the solutions. Their plans can solve complex economic concerns, educational concerns, foreign relations concerns, terrorist concerns, and so forth.

Of course, we should all know from history that things do not get significantly better simply because of the election of certain candidates. Most major tasks are a whole lot more complex and difficult than they may appear to be on the surface. So, while I may not expect that any of the concerns we face in the United States will be able to be addressed in dramatic and positive ways by those running for public office, I will continue to pray for this country and for all who serve it, knowing that our loving God is the only One who is fully capable. Let's continue to pray, in Jesus name, for our country.

Prayer thought: O God, ruler of all things, we thank you for those who serve in public office in our country, but we know they are powerless without your blessing to accomplish purposes pleasing to you. Bless them and our country, for Jesus' sake. Amen.

No Expiration Date

I have a listener friend who sent a wonderful and thought-provoking note about expiration dates. Those dates appear on many of the things we buy today. On perishable items especially, it is always good to check the expiration date.

What my listener friend said was that Christians are especially blessed because there is no expiration date on God's love. It is always there. He gives it graciously and generously no matter what. There is never a need to check the expiration date, because there is none. God is with us through good days and bad days, through bright times and dark times. There may not be many things we can completely count on in this world, but we can always count of God's goodness. There may be many things that get stale, fade away and become worthless, but God's love will never fade away. In fact, it will last for all eternity.

Prayer thought: "For great is his steadfast love toward us, and the faithfulness of the Lord endures forever" (Psalm 117:2). Though faith in Jesus Christ, O God, we know this to be true and we praise you for it. Amen.

FAMILY REUNION

By the way, are you in a family that regularly plans and holds family reunions? Some families have rather elaborate events. Others just an afternoon picnic. Some families never gather, even though the family members may live quite close to one another.

Some families have just grown apart. Some families have histories that seem to keep individual members and family units at odds. Some, perhaps, just see no benefit.

Other families find their extended family to be a strong and life-long base of love and support. This is the kind of family I pray you have. But if not, why not try to reconnect. And don't wait. Make it a priority. Make a call, write a note, send an email, buy a card, drive the miles. God's gift of family is just too precious and too powerful to overlook or neglect. Who knows what blessings may be in store.

Prayer thought: Heavenly Father, you have called us to be brothers and sisters in Christ, members of your family. You have also placed us in earthly families. Help us experience the joy of those families, as well. In Jesus' name. Amen.

RICH INDEED!

Maybe a bigger house would be nice. I could use a new car – especially one with good gas mileage. There are so many places in the world I would like to see. It would be nice to travel…or retire early…or have nicer things…or have more time for the things I enjoy doing.

Does any of that sound familiar? Sometimes people with meager financial resources wish they could be "rich." And it's good to be reminded that most of us are rich…we just don't have a lot of money. What makes us "rich" are things such as family and friends, more comforts and better health than our parents and grandparents, many more conveniences … and, for many of us, the most valuable possession of faith in Jesus Christ. We may not have a lot of money, but we are "rich," indeed – even without all those things we think would be nice to have!

Prayer thought: Loving God, your kindness to us is beyond measure. You have given us so much. Forgive us for always seeking more and lead us to recognize how blessed we are. In Jesus' name. Amen.

GRANDCHILDREN

By the way, if you're a grandparent, you can identify with this. My wife and I have a number of grandchildren, and they are smart, talented, beautiful, and charming – to mention just a few of their outstanding characteristics. I know that is what many grandparents say about their grandchildren, but in our case, we are not exaggerating.

Reminds me of the conversation two women were having. One was talking almost nonstop about her granddaughter. My granddaughter this…and my granddaughter that. At which point the other woman interrupted and said, "Before you go on too much longer I have to warn you that I have nine grandchildren."

It's wonderful when grandparents take delight in their children and grandchildren. God takes delight in them, too. After all, He created them.

Thanks, God, for the love and care shown by loving families and thanks, especially, for your loving care.

Prayer thought: Dear Father in heaven, you chose to share your grace and blessing to all generations, and you kindly gave the gift of parents and grandparents who pass on your great love. We thank you, in Jesus' name. Amen.

WE BELONG

By the way, to what do you belong? To whom do you belong? Belonging is important. It helps define who we are and how we fit in. In fact, belonging may be one of the strongest desires of human beings. We satisfy that desire in a variety of ways. We may belong to organizations, clubs, societies, alumni groups, neighborhood associations and so forth. We may be members of a church. And, of course, for most of us, belonging in a family is very much a part of our lives.

The most powerful and meaningful "belonging" of all comes from a gracious God. He tells us in His Holy Word that "we are His." He chose us. He calls us by name. We belong to His family. We are brothers and sisters of Christ who made it all possible. Thanks, Lord. How blessed we are to belong!

 Prayer thought: Gracious God, you created us. You have called us by name. We belong to you. Lead us to always recognize how eternally fortunate we are to be part of your family, for Jesus' sake. Amen.

He Drew The Map

The story of Christopher Columbus is one of the early history lessons children learn in school. We all know the story, and we all know what happened as a result. We know when he set sail from Spain that he did not know with any precision where his journey would lead.

Think of some of the journeys in your life. Going off to first grade, or high school, or college. Or starting a new job or moving to a new location or joining the military. How about moving into a retirement community or into a nursing home? So many journeys, and we can't know with any certainty where they will end. But God knows where we are going. And while we cannot know what lies ahead, we can be sure there will be discoveries along the way. We know God will provide blessings, and that, if we place our trust in Him, He will happily lead.

Prayer thought: O God, we know not exactly where our journey through life will lead or what we will encounter along the way. We do know that we will never journey alone. You will be with us every step of the way. For this we praise you. Amen.

Expressing Thanks

B y the way, don't you just love how expressive children are? They're seldom reluctant to let others know how they are feeling, whether it is pure joy or pure frustration.

As we "grow up," we tend to become less expressive. For many, the proverbial "poker face" is a virtue. It's not widely popular to wear your feelings on your sleeve.

When Jesus was on earth, He did not communicate with bland and expressionless words, but with feeling. When confronted with sin, disobedience, and rebellion, He expressed His anger and His judgment. He expressed forgiveness to those who repented. He expressed hope to those who were despairing. He expressed joy to those who were sad. And in the face of death, He expressed life.

Thanks, Lord, for helping us to know your love, care, and concern for us and for all people. Lead us to express our true thanks!

Prayer thought: O Lord, there is so much for which we can be thankful. Along with the psalmist, inspire us to be those "…proclaiming thanksgiving aloud and telling all your wondrous deeds" (Psalm 26:7). In Jesus' name. Amen.

Praise Through Music

In the Old Testament of the Bible, David is known for the many Psalms he wrote – Psalms that were musical pieces. David's favorite instrument was the harp, and he gave expression to the deepest feelings of his heart and soul in musical settings that gave praise to Almighty God. We still have that opportunity in a variety of ways.

Perhaps you've been gifted with musical ability. Many of us admire those with such ability. We love to listen to a good choir and to those who are adept at using musical instruments. Many of the hymns in worship convey beautiful messages in powerful ways. The sounds of the organ and strings and percussion and brass are inspirational. And the best of all musical expressions are those that testify to God's greatness and to the blessed gift of faith in Jesus Christ. Whether you are performing or just listening, may God be praised!

Prayer thought: Lord God, you gifted us and your church with many ways to offer praise and honor to you. We thank you for music that is an especially delightful way to communicate that praise in Jesus' name. Amen.

Happy Birthday!

By the way, have you recently had, or are you anticipating, a birthday? I read a little saying recently that really made me chuckle. "Birthdays are good for you. Statistics show that the people who have the most of them live the longest."

Other "statistics," as it were, suggest that those who take life too seriously may actually have fewer birthdays. Life becomes too much of a burden for them. There's something about a good attitude that may not only make life more enjoyable, it may actually lengthen it.

Having a loving God who cares, who has the whole world in His hands, who has a plan for our lives, and who has promised an eternal retirement for those with faith in Jesus Christ – having a loving God like that certainly helps us to maintain a positive perspective. So, may God bless you with a good attitude and with optimism today.

Prayer thought: With all the wonderful things you have provided for us, Heavenly Father, we have ample reason to be joyful in our thinking and acting. Lead us to live positive lives, for Jesus' sake. Amen.

IMMORTAL

Vincent Van Gogh, the well-known artist of the 19th century, studied for a while to become a pastor before he took up art. During his own lifetime he achieved very little recognition or fame. His art was acknowledged, but not necessarily applauded by the critics of the day. It was only after his death that his works came to be well known and quite valuable.

At one point in his life he spoke eloquently about the creativity and artistry of Jesus Christ. "Christ," Van Gogh said, "made no statues, no pictures, and He wrote no books. But what He did make – the crowning artistic achievement of all time, as it were, - was to make living men, immortals." What a truly profound observation! It's true, through His death, Jesus Christ created a path for all those with faith in Him to be immortal. No earthly creation is more beautiful than that!

Prayer thought: Lord Jesus, you "…abolished death and brought life and immortality to light through the gospel…" (II Timothy 1:10). We praise you for the promise of immortality - life forever with you in heaven. Amen.

FUTURE BLESSINGS

The young 3-year-old girl was saying prayers with her father at bedtime. It was just before Christmas. "Thank you, God, for mommy and daddy and brother Sam." There were a few other "thank yous" and a few other thoughts, as well. Then she prayed, "Thank you God for the Christmas lights on my play house outside…that dad hasn't put up yet." Talk about a trusting little girl. Rather than complain that Dad, who promised to put up lights, had not yet done so, she thanked God, knowing that her Dad would keep his promise.

I don't even thank God as often as I should for all His blessings of the past. I don't think I ever thank Him for blessings not yet received. But all of us could do that. He promised never to forsake us.

So, thanks Lord Jesus for all the blessings you yet have planned for me and others here on earth and those planned for all eternity!

Prayer thought: Loving Father, you have assured us in many ways that you love us and that you are our eternal Father who will always keep your promises. We thank you, in Jesus' name, for all the blessings yet in store for us. Amen.

THANK GOD FOR TODAY

I look at the calendar…and then I look in the mirror… and then I conclude that it's probably appropriate that I spend less time looking in the mirror. "Who is that aging person?" I might wonder. "Can't be me, because I don't feel 'old.'" But it's OK, really. Every part of life brings some new challenges we may not welcome. At the same time, it brings new joys and new insights.

Whatever age you happen to be, you can praise God for the life He has given you. You can praise Him for all the joys you have experienced. Don't waste time wishing you could be younger, or older, or smarter, or less forgetful, or less wrinkled. Make the most of this stage in your life. Thank God for today – this day He has graciously given you. And thank Him for the promise of a life to come where age will forever lose it meaning.

Prayer thought: Creator God, you formed us and gave us life. Forgive us for not always appreciating that gift and living life to the fullest. May this day be one for which we can, indeed, be thankful. In Jesus' name. Amen.

LIVING GIFTS

It is true at various times of the year, but it is always in the spring that I find myself talking about the beauty and wonder of nature. I never tire of the forsythia, the daffodils, the roses, the azaleas. I may tire of the dandelions, but even they are miraculous signs of returning life. Given scientific advances, we do have the ability to destroy dandelions, but we could never create them.

The reality is that we human beings have become quite proficient at destroying life, if we choose to do so, but have never been able to create life without the basic building blocks of life. That is something only God has done and continues to do. Life is a very precious gift. Yours is extremely valuable. Take care of it. Treasure it. Thank God for it. And as you are able, use it to support, strengthen, protect and make even more beautiful the living things that are all around you.

 Prayer thought: How glorious are the things you have created, Lord God. How marvelous is the life you have given. May we, as your children, devote our lives to thankfulness and doing those things that honor you, for Jesus' sake. Amen.

A Cure

It was in the year 1928 that a Scottish physician was knighted by the Queen of England. A year later, he won the Nobel Prize for medicine. Obviously, he must have done something quite significant.

As a physician, Alexander Fleming was haunted by the fact that most soldiers who were wounded in World War I died from infection rather than from the wounds that had been inflicted. There had to be a way to minimize the devastation of infection. His hard work led to the discovery of penicillin.

We continue to pray for other such discoveries that will save the lives of those who suffer serious illness. We thank God for discoveries such as penicillin and for the people willing to go the extra mile to uncover them. Also, we thank God for the eternal "cure" He has offered all of us through a Savior, Jesus Christ – a cure guaranteeing life everlasting.

Prayer thought: Lord Jesus, because of our sinfulness, we are destined to suffer as long as we live on this earth. Yet, because of your death and resurrection, an eternal cure has been provided through faith in you. How blessed we are! Amen.

CONTENTMENT

I'm always struck by, and a bit envious of, how content a baby is when newly diapered, fed, and ready to go to sleep. It's quite a bit more difficult to find that kind of contentment as we grow older. We're too aware of all those things that detract from contentment. Still, contentment is possible.

Part of contentment, it seems to me, is being close to someone we love and trust. A newborn instinctively learns to trust Mom and Dad and grandparents and other care-givers. If we have been blessed as adults with family and friends we love and trust, and we can be close to them, it may be easier to be content. If we truly feel the closeness of our loving God in Jesus Christ, who cares for us in ways beyond our ability to comprehend, then in any circumstance we can find some real peace and contentment.

 Prayer thought: Dear God, you have assured us that you will be close to us at all times and in all places. Your kind care and closeness bring comfort, courage and hope. For surrounding us with your love we thank you, in Jesus' name. Amen.

Outlook Or Up-Look?

O ne of my favorite memories of being a father is the memory of my young children looking up at me with their beautiful, young, longing eyes to tell me something, to ask a question, or to ask for help. Of course, the dependence upon Dad disappears a bit as children grow, but looking to others is something all of us do in one way or another for all of our lives. We can't make it entirely by ourselves. We depend upon others.

Some wise person has suggested that a key to happiness and peace in our lives is not so much our "outlook," but our "UP-look." Think about it. We are so much more dependent upon our loving God than any child is ever dependent upon an earthly father. We still have questions. We still need help. We still need to be loved and accepted. Thank God, we can still look UP!

Prayer thought: Forgive us, dear Father, for the times we fail to look to you for strength, hope, forgiveness, and care. Tilt our eyes upward to see more clearly those things you would give to us for Jesus' sake. Amen.

JUST AS I AM

Perhaps you know an old and dearly loved Christian hymn titled "Just As I Am." It speaks well of how incapable we are of earning God's love, grace, and favor. There is nothing we can do to earn for ourselves a place in God's heaven. As unworthy as I am, Christ's "blood was shed for me," as the person who wrote it expressed in her hymn.

The hymn was written by someone who knew about frailty. Because of a serious illness she encountered when she was just a young woman, she spent the last 50 years of her life as an invalid. Charlotte Elliott, who authored the hymn and many devotionals, died in 1871. But her testimony to God's love and strength and hope for the future has endured all these years – a tribute to her faith…and a greater tribute to the God who loves each of us so much – know well just who we are.

Prayer thought: Lord Jesus, I have done so many things to offend you. My sins took you to the cross where you sacrificed yourself for me. Despite my sinfulness, you love me. Thank you for your incomprehensible love. Amen.

SOMEONE IS WATCHING

Surveillance. Something that is very much a part of our lives. Traffic cameras, security cameras, and an increasing number of devices track so many of our comings and goings...not to mention how many of our on-line and phone communications are available to others.

As unsettling as it may be, there is one example of "being seen" that can be a very good thing. The God who created us has kept a watchful eye on us wherever we have gone for however long we have been alive. He has seen all of our failings. He has seen us with our aches and pains, our longings, our trials...listened to all that we have spoken... known our thoughts...shared our sorrows. We can all be glad He's watching...because there is not a minute of our lives that we don't need His help and blessing.

Prayer thought: Almighty God, you know and see everything. How fortunate we are that your love and your caring watchfulness extend to everything we do. For Jesus' sake, lead us to think and do what is pleasing to you. Amen.

EVER-PRESENT HELP

Perhaps you know the name Isaac Watts, a truly great hymn writer. We're told that, as a child, he often spoke in rhymes. He began to write hymns for the church in his late teens and he later became a preacher.

Even though he constantly wrote hymns of praise, he was sickly as a child, nearly dying of smallpox when he was a teenager. He was very short in stature. He never married. He spent the final years of his life as an invalid. One would hardly expect such a person to write hymns of praise.

During his lifetime, he wrote more than 600 hymns. "O God Our Help In Ages Past" is a very well known one. In it he praised God "for all our comforts here, and better hopes above." Watts knew that when we praise God, our own shortcomings lose their significance. What a wonderful thing to learn!

Prayer thought: We praise you, Dear God, for being "...our refuge and strength, an ever-present help in trouble" (Psalm 46:1 NIV). You have been there in the past and you are our hope for years to come. Accept our thanks, in Jesus' name. Amen.

FREEDOM TO SERVE

We in the United States are familiar with the phrase "land of the free." Indeed, we are blessed with freedom, as misunderstood as that concept may be at times. For some, freedom has been interpreted to mean the license to do whatever they choose. That understanding can lead to all sorts of problems, and even harm to others. Even some of the early colonists in our country refused to defend the young country in which they lived, and some refused to pay taxes. Their reasoning? Freedom.

Freedom, of course, requires a great deal of discipline and carries with it much responsibility. More often than not, it is freedom to exercise responsibility, not freedom from doing so. For us, it's always appropriate to pray for this "land of the free," and to seek God's help and guidance as we strive to be citizens worthy of living in freedom.

Prayer thought: Teach us. Lord God, to value the gifts of freedom and to use the freedom we have been granted to serve those around us and to live according to your will. In Jesus' name. Amen.

No Dropped Calls

In cell phone language, we talk about "dropped" calls – dropped as in "disconnected." Disconnected is not a happy state of affairs. Disconnect is right up there with disrupt, dismiss, and even destroy – all meaning some sort of severing. We feel especially saddened when relationships are disconnected. Sometimes we just lose touch with those who were once close friends. Sometimes we let disagreements disconnect us. Sometimes we lose a friend or loved one in death. Sometimes we are responsible for losing the connection. Sometimes we have no responsibility. Connections are simply broken.

There's one safe place where connections need never be broken! The relationship between God and all of His children will never be disconnected, disrupted, dismissed, or destroyed. Through our Lord Jesus Christ, our connection to God is always open and available. We can call upon Him at any time for any reason. Thanks, Lord, for the connection!

Prayer thought: Lord Jesus, you made it certain for us that we could connect with our gracious, all-knowing God at all times. How grateful we are that nothing can disrupt our access to Him. May we connect with him often. Amen.

NEWNESS

Boy, there's nothing like a new pair of shoes! Or, maybe you would say "a new car," or "a new cell phone," or "a new piece of jewelry."

I remember how thrilled I was as a child with something as simple as a new watch. The old, reliable Timex may have cost only a few dollars at the time, but it was "new" and it brightened my whole world…and it wasn't just a hand-me-down.

I wish I could feel some of that childhood thrill with each new day or week or season or year. There are always new experiences and opportunities, but it seems that not much really changes, and too little really delights. UNLESS…unless we somehow choose to bring about some newness in our lives – a little more time for prayer, perhaps…a little more concern for those around us…a little less taking things for granted…a little less complaining…a little more thankfulness for all the blessings God gives.

Prayer thought: O God, there are times I am convinced there is little new to find in my life. I've been there. Done that. Lift me out of an attitude that keeps me from discovering and recognizing your new gifts every day. In Jesus' name. Amen.

FINISH TO START

Perhaps you've seen a start/finish line with the words START and FINISH appearing on the same line. To look at it, one would not know what competitors might experience from START to FINISH – just that the line is significant.

The Apostle Paul in the Bible talked about running the race of life. *"Let us run with endurance the race that is set before us"* (Hebrews 12:1). Life on this earth, too, has a start line – the day we are conceived. And it has a finish line, the day we depart this life. The distance between the two varies, but in many ways, the START and FINISH are similar. We start life with nothing and can take nothing with us when we FINISH. We have simply completed the "race."

For those with faith in Jesus Christ, however, the FINISH line is exactly where the STARTing line is to a glorious eternity. We FINISH and START at the same place.

Thanks, Lord, for the promise of a new START.

 Prayer thought: When my life ends, O God, it will be the beginning of a new, never-ending life. Protect and guide me as I run the race of the life you have given me, knowing that, because of Jesus Christ, a new start awaits. In his name. Amen.

No Matter What

The well-known and respected chaplain of the United States Congress, Peter Marshall, who died more than 60 years ago, often brought understanding of God's Word to people in all strata of life and society. He was blessed with the ability to make God's revelation relevant and understandable. In one of his writings, he talked about what he called "the greatest miracle of all," and described it in this way:

> "God loves men even in their hate. His heart yearns for us even in our indifference. His pardon and His grace are waiting for us even though we may feel no need of either. And, for Christ's sake, God is willing to forgive sinners such as you and me."

It's true. Despite our indifference and rejection of Him, He loves us nonetheless. How blessed are those with faith in Jesus Christ who will, for all eternity, know the true extent of His love!

Prayer thought: Lord God, too often do I overlook, cover up, and even deny my sinfulness. I am often reluctant to repent of my sins. Even for that, Lord, forgive me. I am eternally blessed and I thank you that in Jesus Christ, you do forgive. In his name. Amen.

UNEXPECTED GIFTS

Have you had some extraordinary experiences lately – special blessings you didn't expect and can't really explain? Actually, that sort of thing happens to all of us many times over, but we often fail to recognize how remarkable the good things are that happen in our lives. We may overlook them, take them for granted, or even try to take credit for them. Still, many things just can't be explained.

As we look back on our lives and the lives of others, it is easy to see that things happened for which we have no explanation. Only God could have made those arrangements, spared that disaster, opened those doors, brought us into contact with those people, put us in that right place at just the right time.

We may not always understand God's plan, but by faith in Jesus Christ, we can know with certainty that His plan is a good one.

Prayer thought: O God, the plans I seek to design for myself too often end in disappointment. In Jesus Christ, let me look to you and seek to discover the many worthwhile plans you would have me follow. Amen.

WONDER OF WONDERS

By the way, as you look around you, do some things amaze you? We may not always recognize or acknowledge things that are amazing, but there really are a lot of them. It's good to take notice. After all, God has provided so many wonders for us to observe and experience. But there's one thing we often overlook. St. Augustine, back in the fifth century said this: "Men go abroad to wonder at the heights of mountains, at the huge waves of the sea, at the long courses of the rivers, at the vast compass of the ocean, at the circular motions of the stars; and they pass by themselves without wondering."

The crowning accomplishment of God's creation is you. You are a wonder of wonders! Your intricate body, your powerful mind, your astonishing abilities are truly amazing! Today, thank God for the wonder that you are!

 Prayer thought: Lord God, inspire us to embrace the knowledge of how miraculously you made us. We are, indeed, wonderfully made and, by your design, can do wonderful things for Jesus' sake. Amen.

THOSE WHO HAVE GONE BEFORE

F ranklin Roosevelt was President of the United States from 1933 to 1945. Much of the Great Depression and all of World War II happened during his presidency. What a trying time for the citizens of the United States! How important it was for citizens to pull together and remain strong.

There is a monument to Franklin Roosevelt in Washington, DC. It is not as visible to passers-by and not as prominent as the Lincoln, Jefferson, Washington, Martin Luther King, and World War II monuments. It is somewhat unique being a monument not only to a president, but to all the citizens who worked and fought for their country during his presidency. There are so many for whom we should be grateful – those who have gone before, those who contributed so much to our way of life. Lord, let us never forget the God-given strength, resolve, and willingness to sacrifice of those who have gone before!

Prayer thought: Dear God, how easy it is to forget those who gave so much so that we might enjoy the freedoms we have. We thank you for them and their sacrifices. Help us to follow in their footsteps. In Jesus' name. Amen.

THE REST OF THE STORY

It was back in 2009 that one newspaper headline read "The end of the story." It was a headline announcing the death of well-known radio personality Paul Harvey. The headline was written to bring to mind his famous radio segment called "The Rest of the Story." Paul Harvey's ability to unravel a story in interesting and insightful ways was remarkable. Often there was a significant observation or lesson to learn at the end of the stories he told so well.

None of can know yet "the rest of the story" for our lives. Only God has that knowledge. But one day we will know, too. Those with faith in Jesus Christ will have an eternity to spend enjoying "the rest of the story" that God so carefully planned for them. In the meantime, know that God wants to be part of your earthly story, as well.

Prayer thought: Dear Heavenly Father, your plan from the very beginning was to arrange for us, through Jesus Christ, to have a blessed eternity. The story of our lives is not all there is. We praise you for the eternal story you have planned for us. In Jesus' name. Amen.

BELOVED CHILDREN

A young mother gazed into the crib of her sleeping infant and smiled. To her, he was the most beautiful thing she had ever seen. No words could describe the amount of love she felt for her young son. She noticed he had kicked off his small blanket, so with great care and gentleness, she covered him.

What a picture of how God cares for us. He gazes at us every moment of the day. To God, we are most beautiful. No words can describe the amount of love He feels for us. He notices when we have sinned and He hears our prayers. Then with great care and gentleness, He covers us with a blanket of forgiveness, created by the sacrifice of His Son, Jesus Christ.

The sleeping baby may not be able to comprehend how much he is loved. We cannot fully comprehend God's love, either. Still, you can always know that you ARE loved!

Prayer thought: Dear God, what a kind and loving father you are. Our sins offend you, and yet you offer us forgiveness. We are your creation and your care for us in Jesus Christ is enormous. Accept our thanks, in Jesus' name. Amen.

FOREVER FAITHFUL

As you know, there are more senior citizens in the United States today than ever. For many seniors, it can be a wonderful time of life. However, it is also true that being in one's "senior" years is not necessarily the easiest time of life. As the title of a series of writings says, "Growing Old Is Not for Sissies." That, of course, has been true in all generations.

King David in the Old Testament had something to say about growing old: *"I have been young, and now am old,"* David said, *"yet have I not seen the righteous forsaken…"* (Psalm 37:5). What David said is true. God forsakes none of those who look to Him. God is there for us no matter what our circumstance, state of health, extent of mobility, mental capacity…or age. Thanks, Lord! It's nice to know there is one thing we never have to worry about as we grow older.

Prayer thought: Bless, loving Heavenly Father, all those who are living in their senior years. Grant them grace to endure the challenges, joy in the days you provide, and hearts of thanksgiving for your care. In Jesus' name. Amen.

SECTION III

HOPE, COMFORT, COURAGE AND LOVE

THOUGHTS FOR YOUR DAY

OVER AND OVER

By the way, have you noticed that some jobs are never done? It seems I just cut the grass. Didn't I just take the garbage out? I'm sure I just cleaned the kitchen. I thought I just filled up the car with gas.

Some jobs are just never completely finished. Some may become a bit tiring. Others can be great blessings. Take loving and forgiving, for example. As long as we live on this earth, there will always be a need to love and forgive those around us. As we do, those we have loved will be blessed, and they will be more capable of loving and forgiving those around them.

Our God is an "over and over" God. Over and over He shows His love. Over and over our faith in Jesus Christ gives us access to Him. Over and over He forgives. Over and over He assures us of the strength and wisdom to love and forgive, too.

Prayer thought: Loving Lord Jesus, you can make us "over and over" people – loving, uplifting, forgiving, and strengthening those around us…and doing it over and over again. For that we pray in your name. Amen.

SOME GOOD NEWS

B y the way, have you gotten some really good news lately? There's a passage in the Old Testament of the Bible that describes in a visual way the joy of receiving good news. "How beautiful upon the mountains are the feet of him who brings good news" (Isaiah 52:7). When Isaiah was inspired to write those words, he was talking about messengers who ran from town to town and through the mountains to deliver good news.

Today tweets, texts, the Internet, phone calls, radio, television, and other technologies can bring good news. But there are still messengers. A doctor with good news about a medical condition. A child with good news about a report card. Parents announcing to friends and loved ones the birth of a healthy child.

And Jesus comes to us through His Word with the best news of all – life and salvation in Him. What a beautiful message!

Prayer thought: We praise you, Lord God, for the good news you bring to us – through you Holy Word and through those who teach, counsel, and encourage us in our faith in Jesus Christ. Amen.

PLEASE FATHER...

As they were growing up, our boys were pretty good at it. But the girls were especially gifted in the practice of getting Dad to do something special for them. "Oh Daddy, please…" That would be the introduction… and I knew what would follow – the urgent request. I recall one of my daughters approaching me with what she considered to be a "very important" request. And not believing it was really all that essential, I tried to interject some levity and I quipped, "And why would I do that?" And her response was "Because you're my father." She had me.

When we take requests to our Heavenly Father, we know that He always knows what's best, and He will answer our prayers in the most appropriate ways. Still, when speaking with God, it's OK to say, "I bring this concern or request to you in Jesus' name…because you're my Father.

Prayer thought: Lord Jesus, you assured your followers that "…whatever you ask of the Father in my name, he will give it to you" (John 16:23). How blessed we are to have a loving Father! Amen.

THE LITTLE THINGS

The teacher was trying to explain to her students the concept of "loving-kindness." She asked her students if anyone could help the class understand, or give examples, of "loving-kindness." One young man popped up and said "If I was really hungry and someone gave me a piece of bread to eat, that would be kindness. But, if they put a little butter and jam on it, that would be loving-kindness."

In life, it's often the little things that make such a big difference. In the Bible we read of Jesus showing loving-kindness. For us, following the example of Jesus, it may be a visit to someone who is lonely or in prison, the gift of clothing to someone in need, encouraging a friend, co-worker or fellow student who is down, or reaching out to brighten the lives of widows and orphans. Let's all look around us today to discover opportunities for showing some loving-kindness.

Prayer thought: Make me observant and sensitive enough, Lord Jesus, to see the opportunities in my life today for going out of my way to be the one who helps others receive your kind of loving-kindness. Amen.

BELIEVING AND UNDERSTANDING

By the way, do you find yourself saying or thinking from time to time, "I just don't understand?" There are so many things in life that are too complex, too technical, things that don't make sense. It's true in our faith lives, too. When that happens, a good thing to remember is something Anselm of Canterbury said back in the eleventh century. Influenced in part by something Augustine wrote centuries earlier, Anselm wrote: "I do not seek to understand so that I can believe, but I believe so that I may understand; and what is more, I believe that unless I do believe, I shall not understand."

Believing is a gift. It is not dependent upon our knowledge or IQ, but upon receiving the gift of faith. God has a plan and a purpose for us, and in the end it will not be our understanding that saves us but our belief. Faith in Jesus Christ leads us to understand.

Prayer thought: All knowing Father, thank you for the gift of faith in Jesus Christ and for knowing that "...we have received...the Spirit who is from God, that we might understand..." (I Corinthians 2:12). Amen.

THE PAST IS PAST

Regrets. We all have them. Sometimes we blame ourselves: "If only I hadn't...overused my credit cards...broken the speed limit as much as I did...been so hard on my children...neglected my health, been dishonest," and so forth. Sometimes we blame others: "If only I had a better boss...or a better spouse...or a higher-paying job. If only they hadn't treated me so unfairly ...discouraged me...forced me to get into trouble," and so forth.

There are, of course, many legitimate regrets in the lives of all human beings. We regret missed opportunities. We regret tragedies that have occurred in our world. We regret often neglecting the ones we love. Still other regrets are nothing more than the blame game – blaming other people and circumstances for our own problems. With God's help, each of us can get beyond regrets and blaming and move on to demonstrate love, to serve God and our fellow human beings, to celebrate God's goodness. These things are never regrettable.

 Prayer thought: Heavenly Father, forgive us for the many times we fail to live as your children and fail to accept responsibility for our weaknesses and sins. For Jesus' sake, help us avoid regrettable behavior. Amen.

UPHILL BATTLES

The Rockies, the Appalachians, and other mountain ranges are familiar to many citizens of the United States. If you've driven highways that cross these ranges, you probably know how beautiful the scenery can be. You may also know well the steep, seemingly never-ending inclines. You may have wondered if going up hill would actually end – if you would ever be able to go down hill again. It wasn't that bad, of course, but some of the inclines are very long and you find yourself longing for the end of the incline.

This may be the way we sometimes view our current problems. Will they ever end? Is it going to be an uphill battle forever? Well, there are some battles that do go on as long as we live on this earth. But, fortunately, our loving God, through Jesus Christ, has promised strength and endurance. His love and His promises always offer a break, hope, joy, and the ability to "coast" occasionally, knowing we are supported and embraced in His mighty arms.

Prayer thought: In you, Lord God, I have found rest and safety from my uphill battles. I praise you because "...you are my fortress, my refuge in times of trouble" (Psalm 59:16 NIV).

When I Grow Up

I don't know how long you have lived on this earth, but I've known many people in their 40s and 50s and even 60s and beyond who have said they still haven't quite figured out what they are going to do when they "grow up." Most of us find ourselves never completely satisfied. There is part of us that is always looking for something else, something new, something different. There is nothing wrong with trying to better ourselves, to do more to help those around us, to acquire more education, to give more attention to our loved ones. But complaining about our circumstances is a waste of good energy. Constant dissatisfaction with our lot in life is very draining and accomplishes little.

The Apostle Paul, in the New Testament of the Bible, said *"I have learned the secret of being content in any and every situation, whether well-fed or hungry, whether living in plenty or in want. I can do all this through him (Christ) who gives me strength"* (Philippians 4:12, 13 NIV). I'd like to "grow up" to have that kind of attitude!

Prayer thought: Loving Lord Jesus, you know that I am often without the kind of contentment in my life that only you can bring. Give me a contented attitude and a full measure of your gift of strength. In your name I pray. Amen.

BEHAVING

I t's a twist on the old adage of "actions speak louder than words." It was Mark Twain who said: "Education does not mean teaching people to know what they do not know; it means teaching them to behave as they do not behave."

There are a lot of things we know – things that call us to action but we fail to act. We know about healthy lifestyles, but do not always act accordingly. We know about need to be conservative in our use of energy, but do not always act accordingly. There are so many examples.

Many of us know of God's commandments, and the many ways Jesus taught us to live according to God's will, but do not always act accordingly. God expects that we will strive to live as He would have us live. If you need to know more about God's will, study His Word. If you need a stronger resolve to behave accordingly, pray for God's help, direction, and strength.

Prayer thought: Heavenly Father, continue to remind us what we have learned and to heed these words – "…as you received Christ Jesus our Lord, so walk in him…just as you were taught" (Colossians 2: 6, 7). In his name we pray. Amen.

WAITING

Why is the wait so painfully slow? When will we know? How bad is it going to be? Will I be able to handle the news if it is really bad?

Maybe you've spent time in an emergency waiting room or in some other situation where questions like that have run through your mind. At times like that, little else matters. While we continue to hope and pray for good news, we are painfully aware that the news may be anything but good.

Our hearts goes out to all those who may be facing such a situation today. At the same time, our prayers go heavenward to the Lord of life and health and strength and peace. He does care. He knows what people are going through. And He can bring good from situations that seem to us to be the worst.

Oh Lord, bless the troubled hearts with Your presence and show us how we might be able to help.

 Prayer thought: Lord Jesus, you said "Peace I leave with you, my peace I give to you. Let not your hearts be troubled, neither let them be afraid" (John 14:27). Fill troubled hearts everywhere with your peace. Amen.

LIGHTEN YOUR LOAD

If you've ever moved after living in the same place for quite a number of years, you may recall saying something such as "Wow, I forgot how much stuff we have accumulated through the years!" Or, "I can't believe we still have all these things."

Some people are better at cleaning and organizing than others. Some people choose to save very little. Others find it hard to throw anything away or even to give it away. Someplace in between, I suppose, is a happy medium.

That's true in our lives, as well. Some attitudes and habits and beliefs are worth saving at all cost. Some probably should be abandoned. It's not easy to give up the negative attitudes, the bad habits, and the other things not pleasing to God. But what a difference it can make. Among other things, getting rid of all of that can make it much easier to get our lives truly "moving."

Prayer thought: Your Word, Lord God, directs us to "…put away all malice and all deceit and hypocrisy and envy and all slander" (I Peter 2:1, 2). Rid our lives of all those attitudes and behaviors that should not be saved. We pray in Jesus' name. Amen.

Re-Focusing

I get so depressed sometimes." There may be some human beings that have never said anything like that, but it's likely that their number is quite small

There are many circumstances in our lives that lead us to be down and out. We find it difficult to think of anything else. Sometimes it may even be the kind of depression that is totally debilitating

While many of us have never experienced the more severe type of depression, there are times when things seem rather bleak. Could it be that the bleakness is the result of thinking too much of ourselves and the current problem? What could help us move out of that state is getting involved in something that takes our minds off of ourselves and the current problem. A good place to start is to say "Lord, help me get outside myself. Fill my mind with some new thoughts. Give me a worthwhile job to do. Help me move on."

Prayer thought: "Set your minds on things that are above…" (Colossians 3:2). This is what you called us to do, Lord God. Give us the strength to do so – to move beyond what has us dwelling only on our own concerns. In Jesus' name. Amen.

FALSE EVIDENCE APPEARING REAL

Fear not! I don't know how many times that phrase is recorded in the Bible, or how many times Jesus Himself spoke those words, but the numbers have to be sizable.

There are a lot of things going on in our world that are downright frightening – things outside our control. In fact, we may feel powerless to do anything about most of them. The fear we experience can change our lives and keep us from living life to the fullest. Still, God says to us, "fear not." When He does, He is not saying "don't be concerned." He is not saying "don't be aware of your surroundings." He is not saying "don't care about your welfare and that of those around you." He is saying that He is in control. He has promised us eternal protection. He can overcome. Through Jesus Christ, He can assure us of His power in all circumstances and through faith in Him, we can actually fear not.

Prayer thought: Almighty God, your power is far beyond what we can imagine and you can bring it to bear on those things that have us fearful. We pray for that in Jesus' name. Amen.

FREE FROM GUILT

If you can't get a person's attention in any other way, try guilt. For most of us, guilt is one of the hardest things to banish from our lives. It lingers. It haunts us. It saps our strength. It frustrates. Guilt is a weight that slows us down.

There are many, however, who have moved very effectively beyond the kind of guilt that gets in the way of accomplishing important things in life. Think of Peter, a disciple of Jesus Christ, who denied Christ at the time of Christ's trial and crucifixion. His guilt led him to leave the scene, find a quiet place, and weep. Yet, when he came to realize forgiveness from Christ, he became one of the greatest witnesses to Christ of all time. Peter was able to move beyond debilitating guilt.

God does offer forgiveness through Christ. It's a great gift. It's freeing. It's energizing. It allows us to set the guilt aside and concentrate on much more important things.

 Prayer thought: Lord Jesus, you sacrifice on the cross for us was the payment for our sins. We admit those sins and now ask that you would graciously free us from all lingering guilt. We pray it in your most holy name. Amen.

NEVER FORSAKEN

By the way, what are some of the things in our world that can bring a tear to your eye? Perhaps one of the things that touches your heart is the sight of children being abused, neglected, or abandoned. Children are so often the innocent victims, unable to change what is happening to them. Most of us will never know how devastating that can be. Separation, loneliness, and neglect will affect many children for a lifetime.

Of course, adults can feel abandoned, too. Divorce can bring feelings of alienation, abandonment. Serious illness often separates. Many in nursing homes feel forgotten. And we can help. We can reach out to the young and old alike who are "abandoned." We know that a loving God cares for them – a God who has said the He will never leave them or forsake them. As we remember them and express our care for them, we serve as God's messengers with the message "You have not been forsaken!"

 Prayer thought: What great assurance you have given, O God, with these words: "…for the Lord your God goes with you; he will never leave you nor forsake you" (Deuteronomy 31:6 NIV).

TOGETHER IN SUFFERING

"You have my sympathy." That's a very well intentioned expression, and it is among the most common in situations of grief. It's a phrase intended to help those who are suffering know that they are not alone.

If you really understand sympathy, and you are able to fully express it, it can be a wonderful blessing to others. The word itself comes from two Greek words that literally mean "with" or "together in suffering." When you truly sympathize with someone, you are actually suffering, too.

In many ways, only those who have known first hand your type of suffering can truly sympathize. And once you have suffered in a certain way, you can truly sympathize with another going through a similar situation. Jesus suffered greatly. It's no wonder He can and does sympathize with us. Knowing how meaningful sympathy can be in the lives of those who are grieving, He encourages us to express and to show sympathy.

Prayer thought: Lord Jesus, you sympathize with us when we are suffering. We thank you for that and ask that you help us show the love that is in our hearts to those around us who are suffering. In your name. Amen.

WHILE WE WAIT

By the way, how impatient are you? Are you comfortable waiting patiently for things to happen, or are you the kind of person who wants things to happen quickly? It probably depends, in part, on the nature of the thing for which you are waiting.

We may see the completion of some things quickly. Others take a long time. After all his time with the Children of Israel leading them out of Egypt, Moses never got to see the promised land. King David never got to see the temple he wanted to build. Sometimes we are blessed to see major accomplishments. Sometimes they are reserved for future generations.

As Christians, one of the things we will see is eternity. It is a gift to all those with faith in Jesus Christ. And while we may not be anxious to experience it, it is something we know is already eternally accomplished for us, and something that is definitely part of our future.

Prayer thought: Lord Jesus, you won for us room in the place you have prepared for us – your heaven. We thank you for the promise to us that when our earthly journey ends, we will live there forever. Amen.

MEMORIES AND PROMISES

Chances are you have experienced the death of someone close to you. Whether that experience is a recent one or not, I'm sure it is something that crosses your mind from time to time. The memory of significant losses stays with us.

One of the things that is frequently said to someone who has experienced the loss of a loved one is "Let the memories bring you some comfort and peace." I thank God for memories. Memories can be great blessings, but looking back can never bring as much peace and comfort as looking ahead. Those with faith in Jesus Christ are able to do that. They know the words of the Apostle Paul in the Bible are wonderful words – these words: *"…so we shall always be with the Lord. Therefore, encourage one another with these words"* (I Thessalonians 4:18). Thank God for memories of the past. Thank God for the great promise of the future!

Prayer thought: Almighty Father, our hearts ache from the experiences of losing loved ones. Comfort us with memories of past blessings and heal our broken hearts with the promise of a joy-filled eternity. In Jesus' name. Amen.

RUNNING THE RACE

Many of us have a real admiration for those people who are challenged in a variety of ways but still seem to carry on, overcome their weakness, and accomplish great things. There are so many examples of people with serious disabilities who remain confident and optimistic. There are people who face serious hardships and yet are able to be productive, positive influences in the lives of others. At times we may wonder what it is that motivates and sustains them.

We may never know all the secrets to their success, but we can be grateful for the inspiration they give. Among other things, by the grace of God, they have determined to stay active and not give up. The choice is always there for all of us. We can sit and stew over adversity…or run the race of life that God would have us run – a race He has promised to help us run.

Prayer thought: Lord God, keep me moving. Let me lean on your strength. Open my eyes to blessings you yet have in store for me. Give me a positive outlook for the future, for I pray it in Jesus' name. Amen.

NOT WITHOUT GOD

It was a particularly dry, deserted, and desolate area of the country. It seems a visitor to the area, needing directions, stopped and asked one of the folks living in the area for help. After giving explicit directions to the visitor about roads and distances and landmarks, the person who lived in the area went on to describe some of the territory through which the traveler would be traveling. He said, "It's not God-forsaken, it just looks that way."

Well, thank God that there is no place on earth that is God-forsaken. More importantly, there is no person who is God-forsaken. God cares for all people. God cares for you. No matter what your circumstances, know that God is there. No matter how bleak your prospects may seem, God can bring peace and comfort and hope. Trust Him, and reach out to those around you who may be facing some dry and desolate times in their lives.

Prayer thought: Heavenly Father, take away the darkness that invades my life when I feel forsaken. Replace it with the sure knowledge of your presence and your power to overcome. In Jesus' name. Amen.

TRUSTING THE GUIDE

There I was – sitting and trying to figure out a particular problem – trying to determine the best direction for a special effort. It just wasn't clear. There were a number of possibilities, but it was difficult to settle on the best one. It was then I recalled the words of the reformer Martin Luther. He, too, had moments when he was just not sure where God was leading him. This is what he said: "I know not the way God leads me, but well do I know my Guide."

That is a comforting thought! When things don't make a lot of sense and we are not sure of the future, we can always take great comfort in knowing that we have a Guide – the Lord Jesus Christ – Who knows the way. God, of course, can see the way clearly even when we cannot. He is a Guide Who has prepared a way for each of us and a Guide we can always trust.

Prayer thought: Mighty God, you are the all-knowing God of the universe, "...and for your name's sake you lead me and guide me" (Psalm 31:3). How great you are...and how blessed I am. Amen.

SEPARATION SORROW

L ife is full of "good-byes," is it not! There are good-byes from childhood friends, neighbors, schools, employers, communities. Some are just a perfectly normal part of life. Some are good-byes that are not necessary – separations that clearly should not happen. Can you think of problems, concerns, and circumstances in families, in relationships, in organizations that have led to separation? It's very possible that such concerns could have been dealt with in ways that would have avoided painful good-byes and lingering hurt and resentment.

Is it pride that leads to unnecessary good-byes? Is it arrogance? Is it self-centeredness? Perhaps. But when something truly "priceless" is abandoned…when the separation is truly unnecessary, the pain of separation goes very deep. Whatever you do today, pray that God will help you guard, defend, and protect those very valuable people, things and associations that are priceless so that painful good-byes do not happen.

Prayer thought: Lord Jesus, give us the wisdom, good judgment, and will to avoid contributing to unnecessary and painful divisions and separations. In your name we pray. Amen.

A Cinch By The Inch

By the way, do you occasionally make long highway trips? 400, 500, 600 miles? If you say to yourself at the start of the trip that I have to drive 600 miles, it sounds like a lot. It can be daunting. But if you break the trip up into smaller sections, the task seems less overwhelming. You think about getting to a city some 200 miles away. That wasn't too bad. And then another city 150 miles away, and so forth.

"One day at a time," as they say. Or one mile at a time. We can't do it all at once, but we can do it. In life there may be tasks that seem overwhelming, but if we break them into manageable parts, we can eventually complete them.

So don't give up. Perhaps you're facing some big challenges and opportunities. Ask God to help you strive for those things that are pleasing to Him, no matter how big and overwhelming they may seem.

Prayer thought: For you, Heavenly Father, all things are possible. With your help and guidance, seemingly dauntless tasks can be accomplished…one day at a time. Give us hope and perseverance, for Jesus' sake. Amen.

PAST AND FUTURE

So what about the future? Is it something you think about frequently? The future is that great unknown. Some try to predict it and fail more often than not. Is it important to know the future? In some ways it does help as we live our lives and plan for the future. It's helpful to have some inkling of what to expect. Even though we cannot know the future with any precision, one of the best prophets of the future is the past.

Will there be problems in the future.? Yes, just as there have been in the past? Will there be surprises? To be sure. Will what is true and noble and just often lose? Unfortunately, yes. Will God's love and forgiveness and hope and peace always be available? You bet, just as these things have been ours in the past. Look at God's wonderful blessings in the past and know that there are many more blessings coming.

Prayer thought: You have been our loving God in ages past. Fill us with the assurance you're your love will be part of our future, just as it has been part of our past. In Jesus' name. Amen.

UNCHANGING

Are you a computer wizard? If so, I admire you. I use the computer a lot, but much of the technology still doesn't make sense to me. I'm certainly not very well equipped to solve computer-related problems. (Fortunately, I have children I can call upon.) As soon as I manage to "master" a particular function or piece of equipment, it changes. I got a new cell phone recently. It's great. But it came just as I was feeling pretty comfortable with the old one…so I had to start all over to figure out the new one.

That's not unlike life in some ways. We finally sense we are getting a better handle on parenthood, and the children are grown and leave home. We finally figure out our taxes and the rules change. So many examples. Thus it will always be on earth. That's why it is a comfort to know that we have a God who will never change.

Prayer thought: Almighty God, you know everything. You are the creator of all good things. We thank you that our lives on earth are in your hands and that your promises will last forever. In Jesus' name. Amen.

UNSHAKEN

From time to time we may have days when we feel God has lost all His power, or certainly has chosen not to use it on our behalf. We've seen the destruction that terrorists can bring. We know about violent crime. We've seen natural disasters – storms, tornadoes, floods, and wild fires. We've seen a variety of serious hardship and tragedy in our world. The hardships we experience may be smaller, but we feel the hurt of things happening in our lives, too.

There may be days for you when despair comes calling On days like that it is good to remember a passage in the Old Testament book of Isaiah that brings hope. It is a promise from God. God says: *"Though the mountains be shaken and the hills be removed, yet my unfailing love for you will not be shaken nor my covenant of peace be removed"* (Isaiah 54:10 NIV).

It's true. You are God's precious child and He will love you forever!

 Prayer thought: Yours is truly an "unfailing love," Heavenly Father, demonstrated in so many ways, but chiefly in the gift of your Son, Jesus Christ, who has won for us your never-ending grace, mercy, and love. Keep us faithful to him. Amen.

Best Laid Plans

Tell me, has everything in your life turned out just as you planned it? I would be very surprised if you were able to answer "yes." For most of us, there have been quite a number of surprises in our lives – some twists and turns. Some, actually, were much better than we expected. Some were not so good. And some forced us to re-evaluate our earlier plans and to develop some new ones.

There are quite a few people today who have, or are, changing careers, changing plans. Some have discovered that they climbed the ladder of success only to realize that it was leaning against the wrong wall. I admire those who find meaning and satisfaction in pursuing new opportunities – those that serve people, those that make the world a better place, those that accomplish some new things that are pleasing to God.

Don't be afraid to try something new!

Prayer thought: Almighty God, in Jesus Christ you have made us new creations. Help us recognize the new opportunities you provide for accomplishing your purposes while bringing new meaning to our lives. In Jesus' name. Amen.

DEATH INTO LIFE

It's part of life. It happens with regularity. But it's not something that is easy to discuss. It's death. Death is one of those subjects most of us would prefer to avoid. When it comes close to us with the death of a friend or loved one, it's a sad and unpleasant experience. Still, it's part of a normal progression. From the moment we are born we begin to die. The Christian knows that real life – life without dying – doesn't happen until after our death.

The great reformer, Martin Luther, said it this way: "The life of a Christian, from baptism to the grave, is nothing else than the beginning of a blessed death, for at the Last Day God will make the Christian altogether new."

Death may still be a subject that is not pleasant, but Christians can face death knowing that what follows is the beginning of a life that God will make "altogether new."

 Prayer thought: Heavenly Father, preserve us firm in our faith in Jesus Christ until the glorious day when you will make is new forever. In Jesus' name we pray. Amen.

WAR WOUNDS

One of the truly sad realities of war is the aftermath for soldiers. The nightmares, literally and figuratively, continue. We hear occasionally how many returning soldiers, in desperation, choose to end their lives.

Those of us who have never experienced war up close and personal have difficulty understanding. We never will. We sit on the sidelines, as it were, not understanding, but grieving the loss of life and grieving the reality that some lives are so changed because of what they experienced in war. We pray for peace, but know that conflicts and wars between peoples and nations will continue. There are far too many places in our world where war persists.

Those of us sitting on the sidelines feel helpless, wishing we could do more to help. But whatever we do, let us not stop praying for the peace of heart and mind that comes from Jesus Christ – a peace available to all of us, including those suffering the consequences of war.

Prayer thought: Almighty God, embrace with the love of Jesus Christ all those who have and are living the painful results of war. Give them the peace of heart and mind only you can give. In Jesus' name. Amen.

LOVING THE UNLOVELY

When Jesus was on earth, He spent quite a bit of time with people not necessarily embraced by society or by the religious community – lepers, tax collectors, those who were publicly immoral. He was criticized for it by the "proper" people of His day who claimed he should not associate with such people. Those people did not understand the Lord's mission. During His ministry, Jesus made it clear that He came for all people.

It's appropriate for us to commend all those Christians and Christian organizations today that continue in the tradition of Jesus Christ – reaching out to the disadvantaged, the lonely, the despised, the outcasts, the imprisoned. At one time or another, we may all fall into one of those categories. Jesus loves us still. And realizing what He has done for us, makes the task of reaching out to others a privilege and a joy.

Prayer thought: Lord Jesus, we know from what you have told us that when we reach out in love to serve others, we are actually doing it to you. (Matthew 25:45) Lead us to serve you by serving others…all for your sake. Amen.

BEARING AND SHARING

John DeVries, a missionary and public speaker, tells the story of the fruit tree that carefully piled all its fruit neatly around its trunk. The tree was quite pleased with what it had accomplished and it proudly boasted, "How blessed I have been!." And God responded, "How foolish you are. Your purpose is to bear the fruit and give it away. In fact, at this moment your fruit is being consumed by worms that will soon enter your trunk to destroy you."

Caring only for our own wants and needs can eventually destroy us, too. Healthier and happier in many ways are those who share themselves with others – their time, their words of encouragement, their prayers for others, their gifts in support of God-pleasing causes. And one of the beautiful results is that as we share the gifts God has given to us, He provides a new crop.

Prayer thought: Lord Jesus, you challenge us with the question "…what does it profit a man to gain the whole world and forfeit his soul?" (Mark 8:36) Lead us to "profit," rather, through our service to others. In your name. Amen.

HE MADE ME GLAD

Horatius Bonar, a Scottish pastor in the nineteenth century, was a prolific author. Quite a number of the hymns he wrote are familiar to Christians. His personal life was anything but easy. He experienced quite a number of disappointments and tragedies. Here are some words he wrote:

> I heard the voice of Jesus say: "Come unto me and rest;
> Lay down, thou weary one, lay down Thy head upon My breast."
> I came to Jesus as I was, weary and worn and sad;
> I found in Him a resting place, and He has made me glad.

"Weary and worn and sad." I guess we all have reasons to feel that way from time to time. But the same resting place Horatius Bonar noted in his hymn writing is available to us, just as it was for him. The resting place is Jesus, who always has the power and the desire to help us find "gladness!"

Prayer thought: Lord Jesus, in you is gladness. In the midst of the trials of life that make us weary, you are a safe and secure resting place. Thank you for your love and kindness. Amen.

REST FROM WORRY

By the way, are you spending a day today that is completely free of worry? Probably not. Perhaps you are concerned about all the things that need to be done. Perhaps there are some matters really concerning you. Perhaps it's just that life gets hectic.

A famous King in Israel many centuries ago felt a lot of pressure, too. At one point he wrote these words: *"O that I had wings like a dove! I would fly away and be at rest"* (Psalm 55:6).

But King David could not fly away from his troubles any more than we can. Still, he did find a place of peace and rest – in the caring and comforting arms of a loving God. We can do the same. He's there, wherever you are. He's there to love, comfort and heal – always. When it comes to the "rest" that really matters, you never have to fly far.

Prayer thought: Oh God, no matter what is happening in our lives, you have assured us that we can escape to your loving and comforting arms. Thank you for always being there. In Jesus' name. Amen.

TRY AGAIN

I can't do it. I just can't do it. I will never be able to do it." We sometimes hear children say that as they try something new. Maybe it's trying at first to ride a bicycle. Maybe it's mastering a sport, or playing the piano, or figuring out calculus. You may recall times in your life – as a child and as an adult – when you said or thought something similar.

There are a number of ways to express this sentiment, but it is true, "Those who try to do something and fail are infinitely better than those who try to do nothing and succeed at it."

Overcoming obstacles, making good choices, doing what God has told us is noble and true and just and loving – these things may not be easy. We can choose to not even try. Or, with God's help, we can try. It's certainly a whole lot better than succeeding at failure.

Prayer thought: Lord Jesus, you can make of us people who and not timid – those who choose to strive for accomplishing what you would have us do in your holy name. Bless us to that end. Amen.

OVERCOMING

Perhaps you have enjoyed the music of Ludwig Van Beethoven through the years. Indeed, he was able to compose some marvelous works. Like many greats in many different fields, he achieved some of his finest works in the worst of times. When his health problems were most severe and he faced other life crises, he composed some of his most beautiful music.

It's just another example of God's ability to bring good in the midst of some seemingly impossible circumstances. Maybe you're under a lot of pressure today. Perhaps you are facing some serious difficulties. Don't overlook the fact that this just could be a time when God will help you accomplish something truly significant. God can bring us comfort in times of distress, endurance in times of weariness, and hope in times of trial. Look, today, for what blessing He may wish to bring about through you.

Prayer thought: Lord God, through your kindness, you have gifted me with the ability to do some marvelous things. Open my eyes to see more clearly the purposes to which you are calling me. In Jesus' name. Amen.

BENEATH THE SURFACE

My wife has the habit of writing a lot of things on the family calendar – birthdays, anniversaries, appointments, and so forth. Maybe you have a calendar like that.

If one were to look at our calendars, one could conclude that life is nothing more than a series of activities, as rewarding as those may be. Most calendars do not record any of the other important things in life – the people we met, the new friends we made, the children and others we helped, the beautiful sights we experienced, the joys we encountered, the things that made us laugh. Most calendars don't record God's faithfulness to us and the many times and ways He blessed us. Calendars seldom record the joys and pains of our hearts and the prayers spoken in Jesus' name.

Well, we probably will not change what we list on our calendars, but we can certainly be thankful that life includes a whole lot more than what is recorded on them.

 Prayer thought: Lord Jesus, life may seem to us to be a never-ending series of events and activities. Help us see life, too, as a never-ending series of wonderful blessings from you. Amen.

In Touch

By the way, have you talked with an old friend lately? When you think of all the good times you had with those who have been friends for many years, it really would be a pick-me-up to see them or hear their voices. Yet, while we may think of friends from time to time, we do not often connect with them.

Some wise person suggested that all of us should "make new friends, but keep the old ones. One is silver…the other gold." All true friends are valuable, but often it's the friends we've had for a long time that are the most valuable.

The most "golden" friend, as it were, is our loving God. He created us. His Son, Jesus, earned for us life everlasting. He knew us before we were born, and He has always been a friend. No matter what you do, keep Him as your friend… and remember to talk with Him regularly.

Prayer thought: What a friend we have in you, Jesus. When, in our lives, we truly need a friend, you're always there to listen, love and care. Thank you, Lord Jesus! Amen

Past History

Some wise person once said: "We sail by the stars, not by our wake." We chart our course by focusing ahead, not by looking at where we have been. With all the new technology, ship captains may no longer have to guide ships by the stars, but they still don't guide them by looking backwards. Try driving a car by looking only in the rearview mirror.

In our lives, it is not always easy to look ahead. We're still bogged down somewhat by the past. But we can't live there. There is a future. We can still affect the future. There's precious little we can do about the past.

It's good for all of us to give thought frequently to where we are going. What can we do to make the future even better? What is God calling us to do? Where is He leading us? As we do that, the Lord will surely bless.

Prayer thought: Lord God, forgive me for spending too much time looking backward and not enough time looking forward. In Jesus Christ you can help me look with confidence to the future. Amen.

MENDING THE BROKEN

By the way, do you consider yourself a good "fixer?" When something at home or at school or at the office needs some repair or restoration, are you good at fixing it? Dads, they say, can fix anything. Moms are experts at fixing hurt feelings and broken hearts. Even duct tape gets a lot of credit for its fixing ability.

But what happens when a promise is broken? Can it be fixed? Can you fix a wrong committed years ago that still plagues you?

As we live our lives, we need to be very careful. Let's work to avoid breaking things that cannot be easily fixed. Let's devote ourselves to honesty and integrity. Let's value relationships with others. Let's seek God's help in repairing, restoring, and building up. And when we fail, let's remember that HE forgives, and that He is capable of some marvelous repair jobs.

Prayer thought: Merciful Lord, you can help us be very careful in life to avoid giving in to thoughts and actions that offend you. Lead us to live lives of integrity that honor our Lord Jesus Christ. Amen.

FAMILY TIES

By the way, how would you define "family?" What is it that makes a family a family? Same name? Same parents? Similar genes? Actually, families come together in a whole variety of ways. Families often include biological children, foster children, step children, and those who were adopted. And families that are just a little less traditional can often be as close or even closer than those with similar genes. Love and commitment are not dependent upon genes.

In a way, if you are a part of the Christian family, you know what it is like to be adopted. God adopted us into His family and that means we have brothers and sisters all over the world. We're connected to one another because of the love we have for Jesus Christ, a love that binds us to one another in a way our loving God intended.

Prayer thought: Almighty God, thank you for declaring to us: "I will be a father to you, and you shall be sons and daughters to me…" (II Corinthians 6:18). In Jesus' name, thank you for making us part of your family. Amen.

Words That Last

B y the way, are you swayed by powerful communicators? It seems there are quite a number of them in our world today. Some people just have the ability to motivate people with their command of persuasive speech. Some make a living as motivational speakers. Some are in sales. Some are in government.

Perhaps you've heard a powerful speaker and felt, at the time, quite motivated. But you may have had the experience that after a few days the excitement disappears, much is forgotten, and little has changed.

One of the things we can observe about Jesus during his ministry on earth is that He seldom fit the stereotype of being a strong and powerful motivational speaker or leader. His contacts with people and His teachings were often simple, quiet, gentle, and personal. In fact, that's the way love most often is. And what better motivation is there than love?

Prayer thought: Lord Jesus, you demonstrated your love not with sophisticated rhetoric, but with your death for us on the cross. Help us to follow the great commandment you gave to us – to love others. In your name. Amen.

A GREAT COUNSELOR

B y the way, do you often find it difficult to make decisions?" Some people I've met seem to be very good at making decisions. Some of us are not nearly as good.

"Depends on the decision," you might say. Some have significant and long range implications. They may be big decisions that we have to make only rarely. Some, on the other hand, are quite inconsequential. Butter pecan…or mint chocolate chip? I can't decide. Perhaps I shouldn't choose either, but the choice doesn't much matter. Still, when it comes to the really important choices, it may help to talk with someone, to seek the counsel of someone you trust, and to take your time. More important than all of that is to seek the Lord's guidance. If you're sincere, and you trust Him, you may be amazed at real life directions He can provide.

Prayer thought: Gracious Lord, we pray for the wisdom you can provide to make decisions that are in keeping with your will for us. We pray for that in Jesus' name. Amen.

KEEP THE FAITH

By the way, do you remember how your parents worried about you as you grew up? Perhaps you're a parent worrying now for your children. As the years roll by in our lives, the concern we have for the younger generations seems to grow.

Christian parents have always prayed that their children and grandchildren would keep the faith – that the younger generations would not ignore or abandon the faith. Research indicates that religious knowledge and faith continue to decline in the United States, as it has in many parts of the world.

Fortunately, there continue to be signs that quite a number of young people have faith that is strong and active – those who care about what is right…who care for those around them…who are not ashamed of expressing their faith in Jesus Christ. Thank God for the young people today who set that kind of example!

Prayer thought: Lord God, we are so grateful that strong faith in Jesus Christ is evident in the youngest generation, despite the world's attempt to snuff it out. Protect and inspire al young Christians for Jesus' sake. Amen.

CARE AND CONCERN

I noticed a friend recently who seemed a little distant. It appeared as if he was, perhaps, bogged down in some heavy concerns. But I didn't want to pry, (and I may not have wanted to get involved) so I didn't say anything. And I probably missed an opportunity to really be a friend.

How do you show your concern for those around you? Are you willing to ask how they are doing? Are you willing to listen? Are you willing to take the time? It's not always easy, but I know there are people around you who need to know you care for them. And I know how much it means to you when others show their concern for you.

Let's look for opportunities to "be there" for those around us in their times of need. And let's be thankful for a loving God who is never too busy…and who always cares.

 Prayer thought: Lord Jesus, lead me to be more aware of opportunities around me to show concern for others and to share with them the kind of love you have shown to me. Amen.

HOLD ON!

The musical "Show Boat" debuted in 1927. It was based upon a novel of the same name by Edna Ferber, and music by Jerome Kern and Oscar Hammerstein. It is still a well-known musical. Some find it is especially easy to relate to the song "Old Man River" from the musical – "tired of livin' and scared of dyin', so he just keeps rollin' along."

Do you feel that way on occasion? Tired of living? Scared of dying? Even though the song is very old, the feeling may be even greater today because of the numerous modern-day pressures and threats to our existence.

Even Christians find themselves tired and scared. But their advantage is that they are never alone. "Rollin' on" can have meaning and purpose because of the support and direction of a loving God. Don't give up. There may be some wonderful things waiting…just down stream.

Prayer thought: Lord Jesus, give us the insight to know you have a plan for our lives that can bring joy and optimism, even in a world where there is so much fear. Journey with us. Give us hope. Amen.

HE NEVER SLEEPS

By the way, do you find yourself at least occasionally missing a good night's sleep because of concern about things happening in your life? Some wise person has suggested that we should give our troubles to God…since He will be up all night anyway.

Perhaps you are one of those fortunate individuals that is able to sleep very well…all through the night. But even those so blessed will experience a restless night from time to time. Some problems and concerns and worries do, at least occasionally, interrupt our sleep. We can't seem to shut off our minds. Often, the more we try to overcome the sleeplessness, the more difficult it becomes.

Well, next time you experience one of those nights, remember that God is available 24/7, 365. Not only that, He would like to hear from you. He cares. He wants to share some comfort…and relief…and hope.

Prayer thought: Lord God, the problems we face often seem worse at night. Remind us that you are available at all times and that you long to hear from us. You, Lord, can bring comfort and hope. Amen.

ARISE AND BE DOING

By the way, are there days you feel quite energized? You wake up in the morning ready for the day to come. Other days, it is quite different. There's too much to do…or what you face is too difficult or confusing… or you just don't seem to have the energy. Or maybe it's a much bigger issue – a problem you are facing that keeps you from the ability to get going.

When the Israelites and Canaanites of the Old Testament looked ahead to building Solomon's temple, there was considerable apprehension. And this is what they were told: *"You have an abundance of workmen: stonecutters, masons, carpenters, and all kinds of craftsmen without number, skilled in working gold, silver, bronze, and iron. Arise and work! The Lord be with you!"* (I Chronicles 22:15, 16). The King James version says, *"Arise and be doing!"* What a nice encouragement! "Arise and be doing!" And know that the Lord is with you!

Prayer thought: Lord God, you have gifted us with faith and with so many abilities. Every day we have the opportunity to use those to your glory and the welfare of those around us. May we do so, for Jesus' sake. Amen.

Heart Healthy

B y the way, how's your heart health? I pray it's good in several ways.

In a figurative way, God, in the Bible, talks about the heart being the source of feelings, emotions, desires – both good ones and evil ones. In the "hearts" of all of us (as the Bible defines heart), are thoughts and feelings and desires that are not in keeping with God's will for our lives. In a sense, each of us could use some heart surgery. Wouldn't it be nice if we didn't always have to struggle with temptation and suffer the consequences of our sinful actions? Wouldn't it be nice if the God-pleasing inclinations of our hearts could be more visible?

The bad news is that as long as we live on this earth, evil will be part of life. The good news is that because of Jesus Christ, God can create a new heart within us. Pray for that today.

 Prayer thought: With the Psalmist we can say with confidence, "My flesh and my heart may fail, but God is the strength of my heart and my portion forever" (Psalm 73:26). May it be so for us, in Jesus' name. Amen.

BREAD OF TEARS

There's a somewhat unusual and seemingly contradictory idea in one of the Biblical Psalms – these words: *"You have fed them with the bread of tears"* (Psalm 80:5).

Normally, we think of being fed as a good thing, a nourishing and strengthening thing. It certainly doesn't seem that being "fed with the bread of tears" can be a good thing. But think back in your life and in the lives of others. Are there not powerful examples of good coming from bad situations? Did a particular trial make you stronger? Perhaps. Did a time of great sadness bring you closer to God? It may have. Did a struggle actually build you up so that you were better prepared to face other struggles? Quite possibly. This side of eternity we will all face disappointments, but we are blessed to know that God can bring hope and comfort and nourishment even from the "bread of tears."

Prayer thought: Almighty God, as long as we live on this earth we will suffer disappointment and heartache. We pray that you would lift us from those experiences and assure us of your love and care. In Jesus' name. Amen.

NO EXCUSE

Excuses, excuses! That's all I ever hear," sighed a weary mother of two teenagers. Sound familiar? You've probably heard your share of those in your life, too. And, to be honest, you may have come up with a few of your own excuses, as well.

In Old Testament times, God told Moses to lead the Israelites out of Egypt and Moses had excuses, too. "I'm a nobody," he claimed. "They won't believe me. I'm too timid. I'm not a good speaker." But, as we know, God didn't listen to the excuses of Moses.

We often do the same thing when God calls us. We have a set of excuses, too. "Don't have the time. Don't have the ability," and so forth. But God says that excuses are not necessary and often times they are not valid. Look at the power He gave Moses to succeed. He can do the same for us.

Prayer thought: Precious Lord Jesus, fill me with the desire and the abilities to accomplish those thing you would have me do. Replace my excuses with a strong, new commitment to serve, for your sake. Amen.

PLEASE FORGIVE

In the previous message, I mentioned our tendency as human beings to offer excuses. We may do so to avoid doing what God calls us to do. We do so, as well, to cover up things we should not have done. Do we do that to convince others that our mistakes were not our own fault, or are we trying to convince ourselves?

Fortunately, we have a loving God who even forgives our sins of making excuses. But we need to acknowledge those sins, too – even the ones of which we are not fully aware. King David in the Old Testament said, *"For I know my transgressions, and my sin is ever before me"* (Psalm 51:2). And then comes the good news from God as found in the New Testament, *"If we confess our sins, He is faithful and just to forgive us our sins…"* (I John 1:9).

Prayer thought: Eternal Father, you see through my excuses. When I admit them and turn from them, you forgive. Empower me as I seek to do your will and lead me away from my excuses. In Jesus' name. Amen.

ADVENTURES AT ANY AGE

Age is a state of mind. You're probably heard people say that. Some, it seems, have a much better state of mind than others. My mother-in-law, for example, is still independent and active at the age of 95, living alone, driving her car, and involved in church and community events. And, able to win most of the card games she plays with her children. We should all be so fortunate. But, there are many examples.

Cato was 80 when he began his study of Greek. Chaucer began writing *The Canterbury Tales* when he was 45, and finished at age 61. Michelangelo worked until the day of his death, and even at age 90, his self-portrait was with an hourglass and its inscription read, "I am still learning."

God's gift of life to us can be a meaningful, growing, productive, and satisfying adventure at any age. Pray that He leads you to make the most of it.

Prayer thought: Everlasting God, there are so many things for which we can be thankful at any age. Be gracious to us and help us live life to the fullest, no matter what our age may be. In Jesus' name. Amen.

HONEST TO OUR GOD

No doubt you have heard it said "be careful what you say!" Normally, that's very good advice. Have you said things you later regretted? Probably. We all do it. We've been told that "engaging our brains before engaging our tongues is normally a very good idea."

There is one context, however, in which we can speak freely. We don't have to worry about having just the right words. We don't have to worry that our words will be taken out of context. We don't have to worry that we will be embarrassed or that our words will be used against us by those around us. When we speak with our loving God in Jesus' name, we can speak freely, openly, and honestly. It's OK to express the deepest feelings of our hearts. It's OK to admit our wrongs. It's OK to ask for help.

Let's do so often!

Prayer thought: Loving Lord, thank you for assuring us that you are call upon you at any time and bring to you those things on our hearts and minds. Thank you for always being there. Amen.

IF ONLY...

Boy, I wish I were smarter…or more talented…or had more resources…or… Sound familiar? Do you have a "wish" list, too? Do you sometimes think life would be so much better if only you had *more* of certain things? When it comes to things considered big and important, we may be convinced that we really have "little," to offer.

But think about this: "Little can be a lot, if God is in it!" The Bible is full of stories of God using people who thought they had little to offer. Jesus showed us great blessings from seemingly little things – a cup of cold water, a few fish and a few loaves of bread, a piece of bread and a sip of wine, a tattered band of followers, and a cross.

If God is in your days and in your work and in your plans and in your prayers, some powerful things can happen.

Prayer thought: Almighty God, nothing is beyond your ability. Though I often act as if I have little to offer in your Kingdom, lead me to know that, with your blessing in Jesus Christ, I can be part of your plan. Amen.

CARING AND LOVING

By the way, is your family a pet family? Through the years, our family had a number of dogs. We loved them very much and we discovered something other pet owners have discovered – that dogs, for example, are so smart that from little on they can train people to care for them, provide comfortable surroundings, pet them, play with them, and regularly give them food and special treats? Amazing!

If you love animals, you're always happy to see pets well cared for. And it is pretty easy to see that pets can respond very positively to the love and care given them by the people they have "trained."

We human beings respond positively to love and care, too, don't we? Just as we appreciate being loved, so do others. As God has shown so much great love and care to us, let's work at reflecting that to those around us.

Prayer thought: Merciful Father, direct us to "Put on then, as God's chosen ones...compassionate hearts, kindness, humility, meekness, and patience..." (Colossians 3:12). In Jesus' name. Amen.

GODLY LEADERSHIP

By the way, are you a boss? Do you have responsibility for supervising and leading people? Actually, most of us are in positions – formal and informal – where we influence and lead others. Even if you are not a boss in the formal sense, chances are you have a boss.

There are a lot of management experts around today who have a lot of advice for bosses. Their advice varies widely. There are, no doubt, many factors that go into whether or not a person can be a good and successful boss. Still, the truly good bosses with whom I have worked through the years had several basic characteristics (along with competence) – these characteristics: an appreciation for God-given abilities and opportunities; honesty and humility; kindness and more concern for the task at hand and more concern for those they supervised than they had for furthering their own careers. Frankly, those are good characteristics for all of us in many areas of life.

Prayer thought: Thank you, Lord God, for the many in leadership positions who truly live their Christian faith. Give us opportunities to thank them, encourage them, and follow their example. In Jesus' name. Amen.

LIVING WITHOUT FEAR

Schools, movie theaters, shopping malls and other places have been the scenes of tragic violence. As much as we would like to be able to anticipate such events and intervene to stop them, we know that similar events will happen again. Perhaps you remember the days, weeks, and months following 9-11 when you wondered if and when another terrorist attack would take place. You may have avoided crowded places, tall buildings, and other locations where such an attack might happen.

As much as we would like it to be otherwise, God never promised life on earth would be without pain, suffering, and surprise. So long as we live, we will live in the shadow of events that bring about devastating results. What God did promise was that, despite the many threats, He would never leave us. And He promised that one day, those with faith in Jesus Christ, would have the great joy of living without fear, without pain, and without an unknown future.

Prayer thought: Heavenly Father, guide and protect us as we encounter dangers and unpleasant situations that can be experienced as part of our journey through life. In Jesus' name we pray. Amen.

Simple Expressions

I received an email from a friend with news of a diagnosis of cancer. Unfortunately, that sort of news happens to people around the world every day. I sent an email back to the person, but felt it was such a weak and small thing to do. I wished I could be more helpful and more encouraging. Sometimes we are able to look the person in the eyes and let them know they are loved and that prayers will be sent heavenward. Sometimes distance gets in the way of doing that.

Perhaps you've had similar experiences. It's a helpless feeling. Still, we know that a loving God is there, with the person. We know He cares. We know He can provide the strength to get through the ordeal. And we also know that simple expressions of concern and love from friends and family can be a wonderful boost to those facing difficult times.

Prayer thought: Lord Jesus, wrap your loving arms around those who are suffering with bad news in their lives. Give them strength and hope and surround them with the love of family and friends. In your name. Amen.

Disguised Opportunities

By the way, are you fond of opportunities disguised as problems? Probably not. Fact is, we probably fail to see opportunities when we look at the problems we face. We see the downside, the immediate. It may never occur to us that the problem may actually be an opportunity.

Haven't there been times in your life when a problem has resulted in a blessing? It may have taken a while to discover the opportunity. It may not have been obvious at the moment that somewhere inside the problem was a God-given opportunity.

Whatever sticky issue you may be facing today, just know that God can bring some good from it. Perhaps it will make you rely more on Him. Perhaps it will help you realize what is really important. Perhaps it is not only a problem you may see clearly, but an opportunity waiting to be discovered.

Prayer thought: Merciful Father, in the midst of challenges and disappointments we may encounter, let us feel your loving touch and see the opportunities for wonderful blessings that can result. In Jesus' name. Amen.

Never Alone

There are people in this world who seem quite content to live very isolated lives. Recluse and hermit are just some of the names we may use to describe them. For most of us, it's hard to imagine being so alone. Someone has suggested that loving people around us can cut our grief in half...and double our joy.

Doesn't it help, when you are grieving, to have people around you to help carry the burden? And when something very good happens in our lives, isn't it nice to share that joy with others?

Our loving God is there to do both. He knows our moments of grieving, and He can identify with our grief. He knows, too, those things that bring great joy.

May God surround you with people who are part of your grieving and rejoicing, and that you will always feel the presence of your loving God.

Prayer thought: O God, you are a kind and caring Father. We thank you for those people in our lives who share our joys and sorrows. Help us to be there for others to share theirs. In Jesus' name. Amen.

TLC

Tender loving care. From time to time, we all need that, don't we. The day has not gone well. You're facing some difficult challenges in your life. You've encountered a serious disappointment. You're uncertain about the future. A dream of yours for something good has not been realized. You need some tender, loving care. In fact, even when things are going well in our lives it is nice to know others love us and care for us.

Jesus expressed His love for people in many ways. Often He reached out to those who needed some special tender, loving care. Sometimes He dramatically changed their lives, restored their health, gave them hope for the future, and assured them that they were not alone. Someone truly cared. And, frequently, He reminded people of His Heavenly Father's plan for them. If someone you know needs some TLC today, follow the example of Jesus and share it.

Prayer thought: Lord Jesus, it's hard to imagine life without you. You give meaning and confidence. You console. You provide hope for the future. You love us. Encourage us to share your love with others. Amen.

SUCCESS NEVERTHELESS

In the Christian church year there are days set aside to remember early disciples, apostles, and others. One such day reminds Christians to remember both St. Peter and St. Paul. It's certainly appropriate to thank God for two men who have something in common – being powerful witnesses to the Lord Jesus Christ. But they also have something in common that is much less flattering. At a point in their individual lives, they both denied Jesus Christ. Paul was a persecutor of Christians before becoming a great missionary. Peter, when pressed to confess his faith at the time of the trial of Jesus, did just the opposite. Yet God chose both of these men to accomplish His purposes.

All of us can rightfully admit to offending God in quite a number of ways. Yet He calls to us to be faithful and powerful Christian witnesses nevertheless. If Peter and Paul could accomplish God's purposes, so can we!

 Prayer thought: Lord Jesus, forgive us for the times we have denied you and call us to be all that we can be in proclaiming you. Make us instruments to tell of your grace and mercy. In your most holy name. Amen.

VICTORIOUS

Some will remember the line made famous on a television sports program many years ago. "The thrill of victory, the agony of defeat." Of course, that is not only true for athletes but for all of us. Clearly, we would all prefer the former, and would like to avoid the latter.

Triumph is always held in high esteem. People want to be victorious. They want to succeed in the things they set out to do. There's a definition of "triumph" that is a good one. It is "umph" added to "try."

Try is not a strong resolve. Many of us often say "I'll try." But we fail to do so and the task is not accomplished. Sometimes it is difficult to muster the energy we need to triumph. It's then we need to remember we're never alone in pursuing worthwhile tasks and goals. Our loving God can give us the inspiration and the "umph" to triumph.

Prayer thought: Lord Jesus, you were victorious for us. You conquered sin and death. You triumphed in your resurrection. Grant us the power to triumph in those things you would have accomplish for you. Amen.

OVERCOMING OBSTACLES

Electricity. It's just one of the things we so often take for granted…until the lights go out. No television. The computer is down. Furnaces and air conditioning systems do not function. We worry about the food in the refrigerator.

Back in the late 1800s, a man by the name of Charles Steinmetz helped launch the electrical era in the United States. It was not always easy for him. He left his native Germany for political reasons. He suffered from a serious physical deformity. Yet, he was not dissuaded from pursuing something that has benefited all of us.

We all have reasons why we are not fully capable of accomplishing some things. There are circumstances that hold us back. Still, pursuing worthwhile goals is a very good thing, even in the face of obstacles. God has given to you and each of us abilities that can, indeed, benefit those around us.

Prayer thought: Grant us, Lord God, the desire and the courage to make the best use of the talents and abilities you have so graciously given to us. In Jesus' name we pray. Amen.

I'M SORRY

There was something recently that I was supposed to do and I completely forgot. So I apologized to my wife. And she said, "No, it's my fault. I should have reminded you or left you a note." "No," I said, "it was my own dumb fault. I should have remembered." And she said "You have a lot on your mind. I could have helped you remember."

So there we were – disagreeing over who should take the blame. That's a bit unusual. Normally, we are not inclined to apologize. But how many times in our world do you hear nations, businesses, organizations and individuals saying "I'm sorry?" Often it is more common to hear expressions such as "It's your fault."

Well, many times it is our fault and we should be willing to say "I'm sorry" to our God, too. Because of Jesus Christ, He does forgive. And that brings a whole lot more peace than blaming someone else.

Prayer thought: Forgive us, Merciful Father, for the times we fail to come to you with repentant hearts. Keep us from making excuses and blaming others. Your forgiveness in Jesus Christ is what we need. In his name. Amen.

OUTWARD-FOCUS

The woman who had been happily married for many years was asked how she could remain so positive about her marriage and life in general. Her response? "I stay away from the mirror, the calendar, and the scale." Well, I'm sure there's more than that, but it's an interesting observation.

We all tend to dwell from time to time on our looks, how quickly time is passing in our lives, and how we wish we could be as fit and slender as we once were. While we should always seek to take the best care of ourselves, concern can simply get in the way of enjoying the life God has given us, no matter what stage of life we may be in. Freedom from unnecessary concern allows us to more fully love and care for spouses, children, friends, neighbors, and all those around us. Loving them because of what Jesus has done for us is what God has called us to do.

Prayer thought: It is part of our sinful human nature, O God, that we are often more focused on ourselves than we are focused on others and how you would have us live. Open us to see beyond ourselves. In Jesus' name. Amen.

A Soft Answer

The higher the pitch, the weaker the argument." That is one person's analysis of how to judge the way disagreements are debated. That may not always be true, but often in disputes, disagreements, protests, and the like, one experiences a lot of high-pitched rhetoric.

General Omar Bradley was a famous American World War II General. One of the things he said and sought to demonstrate with his troops was this: "Anytime you have to raise your voice you're showing weakness." Too seldom is high-pitched speech equated with the truth. Truth can be communicated without a lot of high-pitched fanfare.

When He was on earth, Jesus most often spoke in a calm, uncomplicated manner that touched the lives of people. And he spoke, as well, with actions that clearly demonstrated His love and concern for people. We can do that, too – even without raising our voices.

Prayer thought: There are many times, Lord, when "The words of the wise heard in quiet are better than the shouting of a ruler among fools" (Ecclesiastes 9:17). Teach us how we can speak quietly and gently. Amen.

DIVINE OPPORTUNITIES

Before becoming President of the United States, John F. Kennedy served in the military. He was called a war hero by many. When asked how he became a war hero, he is to have responded, "They sank my boat."

You may never be applauded by many as a hero, but there are so many positive things you can do in response to a bad situation. "How were you able to make such a big difference in the life of that older person?" "Because she was lonely and needed a friend." "How were you able to be so highly respected in your neighborhood?" "I enjoyed getting to know and help my neighbors." "How were you able to communicate so well with young people?" "Because life for them is frequently confusing."

Following the example of Jesus Christ, all of us can look at problems less as problems, and more as opportunities to serve.

Prayer thought: Lord Jesus, give us eyes to see and a heart to respond to those who need love, acceptance, encouragement and direction. Give us the will to share your love. Amen.

SELFLESS SERVICE

"Did you notice I cleaned my room and cleaned up the kitchen?" my daughter asked. Well, I did notice, but had failed to thank her for doing so. It was my fault. I should have shown her some appreciation. It's always nice being recognized. But there are times when doing what is right should simply be done without concern for recognition. It's not easy for any of us to show love, do a deed of kindness, speak a word of support or spend money to help our neighbor in need without first thinking in our mind what benefit it will bring to us.

God did a good deed for us – He sent His only Son, Jesus Christ, to save us from our sins. We should thank Him for that, but God had absolutely no selfish reasons for saving us and no selfish reasons for helping us now in our troubles. Thanks, Lord, for all you have done and continue to do for us!

Prayer thought: God of all mercies, fill us with true thankfulness for all the ways you have shown your concern for us and for the forgiveness offered to us through Jesus Christ. It is in his name we pray. Amen.

PARENTS NEED PRAYERS

We had a pretty good rain storm a while back and there was a big puddle in front of our house. It didn't take long after the rain stopped that neighborhood children were riding their bicycles through the puddle. One young man even managed to quite gently "fall" off his bike into the puddle. Did you do that sort of thing when you were younger? Many of us did. And while it always cost Mom more effort to clean the dirty clothes, it was fairly harmless and provided some fun moments – all part of being a child.

For parents, it's not always easy to know what may be innocent child play and what could be harmful. Raising a child is a great responsibility. Let's pray for all parents that they make God-pleasing decisions that allow their children to experience the wonder of life while always guiding them in directions God would have them go.

Prayer thought: O God, as our Eternal Father, you want only the best for all your children. Make of us positive influencers who help to guide the young in ways you would have them go. In Jesus' name. Amen.

ONE MESSAGE – MANY MEDIA

So, what's the condition of your mailbox? The old fashioned type that is visited by a postal employee. Still used? Ours is – the one at home that is still stuffed daily with a lot of printed material. And this is true, despite the predictions we've heard for some time that printed material is becoming a thing of the past in what is becoming a "paperless" world. Similar predictions have been made about radio and television, and yet they remain quite strong (and, for that, BY THE WAY is grateful).

It's hard to know what communication will be like in the future. There will be changes. But we can all be grateful for the many ways our loving God has gifted us with ways to communicate. And, when those ways are used to communicate about God's love for us in Jesus Christ, we can only be most thankful!

Prayer thought: We thank you, Lord Jesus, for all the ways you have helped your children to share the wonderful story of your love and the life-saving plans your Father has for them. Amen.

HONESTLY CONCERNED

I'm really concerned." Do you find yourself saying that from time to time? "I'm concerned with the economy. I'm concerned that some of the nations in our world are becoming less stable and may be real threats to our wellbeing. I'm afraid my children will face some real challenges in their lives." Maybe your worries involve health and safety issues. Sometimes we worry about threats that are imaginary. As one person said, "I have suffered a great many catastrophes in my life. Most of them never happened." Still, many of our concerns are very real.

One thing that can help, even if just a little bit, is to admit that we are truly concerned. Ignoring it or fighting our uneasiness normally doesn't help. Once you admit your concerns, you can turn to the only One who can truly keep them in perspective and give you some peace – Jesus Christ.

 Prayer thought: "When the righteous cry for help, the Lord hears and delivers them…" (Psalm 34:17). Thank you, Lord, for promising that I can bring my concerns to you. Help me do so, in Jesus' name. Amen.

NEVER FORGOTTEN

The first day of school for little Johnny was a real traumatic experience. He was withdrawn, nervous, and the teacher thought he might even be getting sick. So, the kindly teacher found a way to get Johnny down to an office where He could call his mother for some reassurance. The teacher made the call and handed the phone to Johnny, who, for a brief moment, was not able to talk. Not hearing anything on the other end of the line, the mother asked "Who is this?" And the little boy, with tears running down his face, said, "This is Johnny. Have you forgotten me already?"

I guess we have all experienced loneliness. Next time you feel a bit lonely and forgotten, know that you have a loving God who has never forgotten you and will never forget you. He loves you more that you can possibly know and you need never be separated from Him.

Prayer thought: We know, dear Father, that there is nothing that will ever be able to separate us from your love in Christ Jesus, our Lord (Romans 8:38, 39). Thank you for never forgetting us! In Jesus' name. Amen.

THE WAITING PHYSICIAN

The waiting room in the doctor's office was full of people who needed to see a doctor. Time passed slowly. Few, if any, were being called. Patience in the room was wearing thin. It was at this point that an elderly man stood up and headed for the door. As he did, he said wearily, "Well, I guess I'll just go home and die a natural death."

You might be able to identify with the frustration of waiting. Our lives are busy. We have other things to do.

There are times in our lives when we really need to talk with the Great Physician – Jesus Christ. Fortunately, there are no long lines, no waiting, no wondering when He might be able to hear us. In fact, He might be the one waiting to hear from you. He's pleased when you stop by to visit.

Prayer thought: Lord Jesus, you referred to yourself as a "physician" who came for those who are sick. (Mark 2:17) In many ways, we are not well. We need you, and we thank you for your marvelous ability to heal. Amen.

TRUE RICHES

It's difficult these days to avoid thinking about the economy, taxes, and so forth. No doubt you think occasionally about your own financial wellbeing. It's likely true that most of you would say you are not wealthy. Certainly there are so many people who have a whole lot more than you have. But properly understood, there is more that constitutes "wealth" than possessions.

Here's a helpful saying: "Life is tragic for the person who has plenty to live on, but little to live for." The "living for" part really has little to do with the amount of wealth a person has. There are those with and without earthly wealth who have found great meaning in "living for" a loving God in Jesus Christ and sharing God's love with those around them. It is my prayer that you are wealthy…wealthy in the amount of love you have and the amount you give away.

Prayer thought: Lord God, you have made us wealthy through the love we have received in Jesus Christ. Nothing is more valuable and more eternal. Teach us to embrace that love and share it, for Jesus' sake. Amen.

FACE TO FACE

From time to time I visit a relatively small post office in a small city. It seems every time I go I see the same worker. She knows who I am (as she probably does everyone who visits the post office) and is a most friendly and faithful worker. The post office has some automated things, such as a machine to purchase stamps. I seldom use it. It's nicer to say "hi" to the cheerful worker.

Human interaction has really diminished in the last generation. Cell phones for the youngest generation are the way to communicate. It makes me wonder if we are more and more missing the most valuable form of communication – face to face. Among God's greatest gifts are the people around us. There is something to be said for taking the time to talk with them, ask them how they are doing, and speak a friendly word to them. It's still better than a text message or a meeting with a machine.

Prayer thought: Heavenly Father, we thank you for the new means of electronic communication, but lead us to always value the most effective form of communication that Jesus used – personal and face to face. In his name. Amen

OVERCOMING DEPRESSION

You probably know this historical fact, but it is a nice reminder to us from time to time. Quite some years ago a bright and talented lawyer experienced some troubling times of discouragement and depression. In the midst of one of these bouts he wrote: "I am now the most miserable man living. Whether I shall ever be better, I cannot tell. I awfully forebode I shall not." The man who wrote those words was Abraham Lincoln.

Overcoming depression is not easy. We pray for those suffering and ask God to bring people and resources into their lives to help them. We pray that they might know with great certainty that Jesus gave everything He had for them and that He wants the best for them.

Our discouragements may not be the most severe kind, but we, too, need to know that the Lord is there and that overcoming our deepest hurts is not impossible.

Prayer thought: Precious Savior, you said it so well. "Come to me, all you who are weary and burdened, and I will give you rest" (Matthew 11:28 NIV). In our darkest moments, illuminate for us a path to you. Amen.

No Two Alike

It was all the way back in 1913 that the Ford Motor Company began using a new movable assembly line that ushered in the era of mass production. Think of all the changes that have taken place in manufacturing in the years since 1913. We have gotten much more technologically astute as human beings and we benefit from all sorts of advancements. Still, as human beings, we fall prey to many of the same weaknesses and temptations and failings as people did more than a century ago.

What made a difference for people back then and what still makes a difference is an understanding of why we have been created and by whom. We are not the product of an assembly line. No two of us are exactly alike. We pray that people in every age will know their creator, receive the gift of faith in Jesus Christ, serve Him, and look forward to an eternity with splendor and glory that will never be matched on earth.

Prayer thought: Almighty God, your creative hand fashioned us and for each of us one-of-a-kind human beings you have a purpose. For Jesus sake, fill us with the desire to better know and live that purpose. Amen.

"SILENT" SERVICE

His name was Joseph Mohr. He was a clergyman in Austria in the first half of the 19th century. He died at the age of 56 in 1848. Early in his ministry he gave a gift to the church that is still loved and powerful today. It was a poem he had written and at the last minute, he asked his schoolteacher friend, Franz Gruber to write some music for the poem. It was all done rather hastily. But his gift remains today as a wonderful gift – a Christmas gift. It was Joseph Mohr who wrote the beautiful Christmas Hymn "Silent Night."

In relation to his entire ministry, this was a very small act. Yet, it has endured and has blessed every generation since. God may be choosing you today to do something to accomplish His purposes…and you may never know what a blessing it may be for years to come. Today and everyday, look for ways to serve the Christ who inspired Joseph Mohr.

Prayer thought: Lord Jesus, we rejoice that the story of your love is shared in so many ways. May we use the talents and abilities you have given us to share it, as well. In your name and to your glory. Amen.

CHEERING YOU ON

Whether you are a big sports fan or not, you've heard the term "the 12th man." The Seattle Seahawks have really touted the idea of the 12th man and made the concept more popular. The 12th man is the crowd of supporters – those who cheer on the players on the field. We're told the term came from an article written in 1912 in a University of Iowa publication that credited the spirited Iowa fans – "the 12th player" for "winning" a football game against Illinois.

Well, a little encouragement can go a long way. Knowing our loved ones and friends are "rooting" for us in our various endeavors means a lot. And just as we appreciate encouragement, others do too. Look today for a way to encourage and root for another person. And know that your loving God in Jesus Christ is always rooting for you – encouraging you to be all that He would have you be.

Prayer thought: O Father, without your grace and mercy we are nothing. But with your grace and mercy in Jesus Christ, we share the eternal victory he won for us. Inspire us to boldly celebrate that victory. In Jesus' name. Amen.

WRONG OR RIGHT?

By the way, can you identify with this statement? "There is a demand in these days for men who can make wrong appear right." If you look at the world in which we live, you might conclude that the demand is being fully met. Things we know are wrong are made to look OK – promoted as perfectly acceptable.

There are many examples, but the concern is anything but a new one. That statement, "There is a demand in these days for men who can make wrong appear right" was written by the Roman playwright, Terence, in the second century BC. Making wrong appear right has been a trait of human beings, including us, since the Garden of Eden.

Fortunately, our Savior, Jesus Christ, offers to forgive us and to lead us to do those things that are "right." Thanks, Lord. Help us always to avoid those things in our world that are clearly wrong, even if they are made to appear right.

Prayer thought: Lord Jesus, we are so easily taken in by temptation. Things that are wrong appear to be just fine. Forgive us and place within us the gift of discernment to see more clearly what pleases you and what does not. In your name. Amen.

Section IV

Holidays And Special Occasions

By The Way

Thoughts For Your Day

God's New Day

By the way, what are your plans for this New Year? I'm sure you have some. Young people want to plan exciting futures. Many people in mid-life have plans that are not yet realized. Retirees plan exciting futures, too, looking forward to doing some of the things they were not able to do during their working years. Whatever your plans, you've probably discovered that some of them are just very difficult to realize. And some, when realized, can be disappointing.

All of us would experience more joy and satisfaction in life if we occasionally asked the question: "What are God's plans for me?" I know He has some great ones. He said in the Bible, "I know the plans I have for you…plans to prosper you and not to harm you, plans to give you hope and a future." That's good news!

Lord, help me better understand your plans.

Prayer thought: Almighty God, our calendars tell us to begin a new year. This day and every day is a time to seek your grace and guidance so that we might know better how you would have us approach the future. In Jesus' name. Amen.

Celebrate The Light

Today is the day Christians observe Epiphany. Epiphany means "revelation, dawning." What is meant by that for Christians is that the "Light" of the world, Jesus Christ, has come, and now is the time for Him to be "revealed" to the whole world.

A favorite image of the effect of light comes from something Robert Louis Stevenson is to have said as a young boy. In those days, before electricity, gas lights lit the streets. One night as the lamplighter was making his way down the street lighting the lamps, Stevenson is to have said, "Look, Mom, the man is coming down the street punching holes in the night."

Only our Lord Jesus Christ, the true Light of the world, can "punch holes" in the darkness of our world, and only He can truly brighten the dark corners of our lives. Celebrate that during the season of Epiphany!

Prayer thought: Lord Jesus, bless us with the sure knowledge that the light of the world that you are "...shines in the darkness and the darkness has not overcome it" (John 1:5). Make us those who share your light. In your name. Amen.

Martin Luther King Day
Freedom And Justice

This is the day we remember Dr. Martin Luther King, Jr. – a man who inspired many to work for the causes of freedom and justice. And it's a good day to remember all those who prize freedom and justice.

Needless to say, we have a lot of work to do. There is so much in our world that fights against freedom. There are so many persons in power around the world who seek to oppress people and keep freedom from them. And injustice is everywhere. But before you begin pointing the finger at those who are guilty, consider your own practices. Are you always fair and honest with others? Do you prize freedom for the great gift that it is?

Today is a good day for all of us to look at ourselves, and to pray that God would lead us to be champions of responsible freedom and justice.

Prayer thought: Lord Jesus, open our eyes to the ways in which we can be your instruments to honor and respect those around us and to serve them in ways according to what we have been taught by you. In your name. Amen.

Repentance And Forgiveness

One of the great messages of Lent is forgiveness. The Lord Jesus Christ, who went the way of the cross, promised that those who come humbly to Him in repentance, admitting their sins and seeking forgiveness, will be forgiven. We all need that. Try as we may, we can never live life in such a way that all our thoughts, words and deeds are pure and spotless. What a sense of relief true forgiveness can bring! There may still be consequences for our wrongs, but in God's eyes, those wrongs are no longer held against us. Lent is a time when Christians remember that their sinfulness caused the death of Jesus. It's a solemn time of reflection, and it begins on this Ash Wednesday.

The season of Lent is a good time to seek the Lord's forgiveness. We need to do that in all seasons, but there's no reason to delay. Let us seek God's forgiveness today.

Prayer thought: Lord Jesus, we will never be able to comprehend the extent of your love and sacrifice. Still, inspire us to acknowledge our part in your journey to the cross. Forgive us and bless our journey through Lent. Amen.

Speaking Of Good News

I guess St. Patrick's Day always occurs during the Christian season of Lent. In a sense, it is appropriate timing, because I'm sure St. Patrick talked a lot about the meaning of Lent and a lot about what Christian pastors talk about during this season today. Lent reminds us of the willing sacrifice of Jesus Christ for us and of our need to seek His forgiveness and guidance.

St. Patrick was a Christian whose work in Ireland brought many people to Christ. He was very committed to preaching the Gospel. He often used simple illustrations to teach God's truth. He communicated well, and, through the power of the Holy Spirit, people came to faith. Lent would have been a common subject for him leading to the truth of full and free salvation.

Thanks, Lord, for Patrick and for all those who continue to share the extraordinary Good News you have for all people!

Prayer thought: Dear God, through the power of your Holy Spirit, you have inspired many to share the story of your plan of salvation through Jesus Christ. May we be so inspired. In Jesus' name. Amen.

WHO HE IS

Today, Christians observe Palm Sunday, the beginning of the last week on earth for Jesus Christ as a human being. During this week to come, we will remember the things He did. But none of that is eternally significant unless we know Who He was during that week, and throughout His life. Many on that first Palm Sunday believed He came as an earthly King. He would solve political conflicts and make life easier.

While even the people in Jerusalem did not yet fully comprehend Who this Jesus was, we know that He was King of Kings and Lord of Lords. He was, and is, the eternal Son of God, Savior of the world. None of the things we need most and long to have can be obtained without His blessing.

Thanks, Lord Jesus, for helping us know for sure, by faith, who you are and what you have done for us!

Prayer thought: Lord Jesus, by faith we have come to know who you are and what you have done for us. Assist us to treasure the faith you have given us so that we may proclaim you as King of Kings and Lord of Lords. In your name. Amen.

GOD'S BREAKING NEWS

This is a special news alert…" or "Stay tuned for breaking news!" No doubt you've heard that kind of announcement while watching TV or listening to the radio.

This week, this Holy Week, is a reminder of God's "breaking news." It's the news of forgiveness, and reconciliation, and hope for the future, and a promised eternity. What happened that first Holy week was big news, indeed. Some recognized the Christ for who He was. Some began to sense the significance of Christ's mission and plan. Some did not. And the same is still true today.

How wonderful it would be if everyone could accept, by faith, the good news of a Savior who gave everything for them. What a difference this good news could make in our world today! The story is an old one, but for each of us it can be ever new. It's the "breaking news" of God's love for us today and every day.

Prayer thought: Almighty God, through prophets, priests and Kings you prophesied the coming of the One who would be Savior of the world. He came. Inspire us this week as we recall the news of how he completed his mission on earth. In Jesus' name. Amen.

LOVE ONE ANOTHER

Tomorrow Christians will recall the death of Jesus Christ on the cross of Calvary. An ancient prayer of the Christian church for Good Friday includes a description of Jesus Christ as One who was "contented to be betrayed and given up into the hands of wicked men and to suffer death on a cross." The word "contented" somehow doesn't seem to fit. But the use of that word is very intentional.

As paradoxical as it may appear, Jesus was "contented" in His suffering. He was capable of seeing beyond the cross. He knew His mission would eternally affect all those with faith in Him. He knew He was doing it for you and for me. And on this Maundy Thursday, He gave to us the Lord's Supper and a new "maundatum," (Latin for "commandment" or "mandate") – that we love one another. Considering what He did for us, what a great thing to do!

Prayer thought: As you said, Lord Jesus, "A new commandment I give to you, that you love one another: just as I have loved you, you also are to love one another" (John 13:34). Lead us to keep your commandment. Amen.

DAY OF DARKNESS

ood Friday. A day of darkness. Literally, because there was a period of darkness while Christ hung on the cross. Figuratively, because Good Friday appeared to some as the end of hope.

In some Christian traditions this day has been known as "Sorrowful Friday" or "Holy Friday." How it came to be known as "*Good* Friday" is not fully known. But for us, as Christians, it was a "good" day, despite the death and darkness that marked it.

We all experience darkness in our lives. It's been said that "God sometimes allows us to be in the dark to help show us the light." How thankful we can be when we begin to understand God's good purpose for Good Friday and that the light of Easter was about to dawn. Whatever darkness you may be facing, know that Christ died for you and that He wishes to bring to you His good light.

Prayer thought: Lord Jesus, how could we ever fathom the magnitude of your sacrifice on that first Good Friday? All we can do is reverently remember and thank you for bringing eternal light from the darkness of that day. Amen.

SHOUT FOR JOY!

By the way, when was the last time you jumped and shouted for joy?

Remember how joyful we were as children? We knew how to express joy. The simplest things could spark joyful laughter from us. As adults, we may need to rekindle a bit of that joy in our lives.

As Christians, we can express joy, each day, regardless of our circumstances. We have Jesus Christ as our Savior, and we know that we belong to Him forever. Today is a day of great joy. For many, it is the high point of the church year. What happened that first Easter seals God's promises. We remember Christ's victory over death and we say with boldness and joy, "HE IS RISEN. HE IS RISEN, INDEED. HALLELUJAH!"

It's a monumental victory to be sure. It may not make you want to jump up and down…but it would be OK if you did.

Prayer thought: Heavenly Father, fill us with joy as we recall the magnificent victory of your Son, our Lord and Savior Jesus Christ, on that first Easter. Then, keep that joy alive in us throughout the year. In the name of the Risen Christ. Amen.

PRAY WITHOUT CEASING

Some in the United States of America will today recognize or observe this National Day of Prayer.

It was March 30, 1863, that President Abraham Lincoln signed a proclamation that began with these words: Whereas, the Senate of the United States, devoutly recognizing the Supreme Authority and just Government of Almighty God, in all the affairs of men and of nations, has, by a resolution, requested the President to designate and set apart a day for National prayer and humiliation.

We do not need a National Day of Prayer to remind us how important prayer is. We have access to our loving God at all times and in all places. He loves to hear from His children. Still, a day such as this can be a reminder of our dependence upon "Almighty God," whom we know through Jesus Christ, who is "in all the affairs of men and of nations." Let's speak with Him today and everyday.

Prayer thought: Lord God, you are the "Supreme Authority." Today and every day we can pray that you would guide the people of our world to recognize you for who you are and to lean on your grace and mercy in Jesus Christ. In his name we pray. Amen.

SINCERE THANKS!

Some today are observing Teacher Appreciation Day. For many fine teachers, the recognition is well deserved. Teaching is not the easiest profession, and one day of recognition is surely not enough. But what a tremendous opportunity teachers have to make a difference in the lives of children. No doubt you remember some excellent teachers and how they positively influenced you and, perhaps, helped set a direction for you that has had an impact upon your whole life. Thank God for them.

And if you have the chance today (or any day, for that matter) to commend a teacher, do so. So many good teachers hear words of thanks and praise too seldom. They can, indeed, be instruments of a loving God to bring immediate and life-long blessings to children. This is your day, teachers. We don't want it to go unnoticed. Enjoy it and know that many of us are thanking God for you!

Prayer thought: How valuable, Heavenly Father, are those who teach us and the next generation. How valuable are those who help to teach your eternal truths. Bless them and strengthen them in their important tasks. In Jesus' name. Amen.

Ascension Day
Keep On Moving

There was a time in the Christian church that this day on the church calendar was a significant observance. Today, it often goes unnoticed. It is Ascension Day. Forty days after that first Easter, it was time, according to God's plans, for Jesus to leave the earth and to return to His heavenly home.

I can't imagine what it must have been like for those early followers of Jesus to witness His ascension. Surely they had never seen anything like it. Surely, they had never seen anyone like Him. We are told that those witnesses to the ascension stood rather frozen, as if in shock. It took an angel to get them moving again. And moving was something they needed to do. After all, Jesus left His mission to them. And He left it to modern day followers, as well. Today is a good day to celebrate the Lord's ascension…and then, to keep moving!

Prayer thought: Lord Jesus, you have called upon us to be your witnesses in our world – to carry on the mission you carried out during your time on earth. Fill us with the desire to proclaim your Good News, for your sake. Amen.

GOD'S SPECIAL AGENTS

By the way, who is the most over-worked, underpaid, patient, kind, loving, and helpful person on earth? Well, for many of us, the answer is "Mom." And today is her day.

Mothers, of course, do not always have the easiest job. And children do not always express the appreciation for mothers that mothers deserve. Yet, what a great plan God developed!

For you, today could be a day to remember a mother who is no longer here on this earth. Or, your mother may be miles away. Whatever your circumstance on this Mother's Day, take time to say a word of thanks to God for all the blessings He showers upon people through mothers. In many instances, mothers are God's special agents to teach their children about Jesus Christ and His great love. How wonderful

Thanks, Lord, for mothers. Thanks, Lord, for showing us a glimpse of your great love through them!

 Prayer thought: It was your exceptional plan, Lord God, to gather people in families and you intended to bless families through mothers. Protect and care for them as they love and care for us. In Jesus' name. Amen.

THANKS AND GOD BLESS

Some in our country are observing today as a special day to recognize, remember, and pray for those serving in the Armed Forces. It has not always been easy for those serving, both on and off the battlefields. They have been, and are, buffeted by criticism of themselves and the military actions in which they engaged. It is truly our duty to offer the men and women serving, and those who have served, our thanks and our highest level of respect.

If you or a loved one has served, know that many of us are ready, at any time, to applaud your efforts. So many have gone the extra mile for the wellbeing of their fellow citizens. Those of us not serving in the Armed Forces will probably never fully understand the demands and the sacrifices, but we can at least say "thanks and God bless!" We are happy and honored to do so today.

Prayer thought: As much as we pray for peace, Heavenly Father, we know that in this world of sin wars will continue. Surround those in the Armed Forces with your love and care. In Jesus' name. Amen.

GOOD NEIGHBORS

B y the way, what comes to mind when the word "neighbor" is mentioned. We may think of neighbors as true and lasting blessings. Also, we may know that neighbors can be sources of frustration and conflict.

We in the United States can be grateful for the long and positive relationship we have enjoyed with our neighbor to the north, Canada. Today is a special holiday in Canada – Victoria Day. The significance and meaning of this observance for Canadians has changed a bit through the years, and is still changing. But it is a time for our neighbors in Canada to enjoy a long holiday weekend.

Actually, the radio program BY THE WAY is heard in parts of Canada. To our friends of BY THE WAY in Canada, know that you have friends in the United States who wish you well and pray the Lord's blessing upon you and your country.

Prayer thought: Almighty Lord of nations and peoples, guide those who govern and give to the governed the wisdom to be citizens who strive in their lives and in their countries for values and practices pleasing to you. In Jesus' name we pray. Amen.

SALUTING THOSE WHO SERVED

We all love to dwell on happy memories, don't we? The not-so-happy memories, on the other hand, are difficult and we might wish to avoid them.

Today in the United States is a day of remembering. Some will simply celebrate and enjoy a long weekend, but it is important to remember – even the unpleasant memories. We remember the tragedy of war that has punctuated history and that continues. We remember those whose lives were radically changed or even cut short. We remember because there are so many people for whom we need to be thankful – those who have served our country and those who are serving today.

If you are remembering today the loss or injury of a loved one, know that there are those who pray in Jesus name that you can know His comfort. Know that we appreciate the sacrifice. Know that we thank God today for all who have served so well.

Prayer thought: In the course of events in our world, Lord God, we have come to know that there are times when individuals stand in harm's way. We remember those who have sacrificed so much for our welfare and pray your blessing on those who serve today. In Jesus' name. Amen.

A HELPER

Many Christians today are observing Pentecost. Ten days ago, the Christian Church remembered Ascension – the time when Jesus left this earth to return to His heavenly home. Before He left, He promised that He would send a helper, a counselor, a motivator. The Holy Spirit Jesus promised was made known on that first Pentecost – the Holy Spirit who works through God's Word and through the Sacraments of Baptism and the Lord's Supper to strengthen Christians. The Holy Spirit leads Christians to remain firm in the faith. He works in the lives of those who have not come to faith in Jesus Christ, and He leads Christians to reach out to those individuals.

It's a privilege to be involved in the Lord's mission on earth. It's a blessing, too, to know the Holy Spirit is constantly at work in the world and always with us to help accomplish God's plan.

Prayer thought: For the gift of the Holy Spirit, we thank and praise you, Almighty God. May the Holy Spirit be a constant inspiration for us in keeping our faith in Jesus Christ strong and sharing that faith with others. in Jesus' name. Amen.

RED, WHITE, AND BLUE

I t was on this date (June 14) in 1777 that the well-known stars and stripes became the official flag of the United States. The young Continental Congress chose a design for the flag and chose three colors that the Congress hoped would represent the young country for generations to come.

The color red was chosen to be a symbol of courage. White was chosen to represent purity. And blue was chosen to represent vigilance, perseverance, and justice.

When we fly the flag today, let us ask God's forgiveness for all the ways in which we have failed to be good citizens. Also, may the flag be a reminder of those things for which we as citizens of the United States should strive. God has richly blessed us. We owe him thanks. He has showered so many wonderful things on those who claim the flag as their own.

Prayer thought: It's our flag, dear God, and it represents a country whose history has been marked with so many of your kindnesses. As we honor the flag, let us more so honor you for the blessings that have come to the citizens of the United States. In Jesus' name. Amen.

MORE IMPORTANT THAN THINGS

I t's hard to overestimate the power and influence of parents on children. Last month was Mother's Day. Today is your day, Fathers, and you may not need to be reminded of how important you are in the lives of your children.

In the demanding world in which we live, there are so many things we want to do for our children. We want to make sure they are cared for, get a good education, have solid values, remain safe, and avoid dangerous temptations. In addition to all of that, we'd like to think that someday there would be some inheritance for them.

Here's a thought for Fathers (and Mothers, too): "The best inheritance parents can give their children is a few minutes of their time each day." It's during these times that values, faith in Jesus Christ, and love are shared – things that are so much more important than "things."

Prayer thought: Heavenly Father, you are for earthly fathers a model of love and concern. We pray that you lead fathers to look to you as they seek to be husbands and fathers who model your love in Jesus Christ. Amen.

THE GIFT OF FREEDOM

There's so much to learn about the history of the United States. One could spend the rest of his or her life simply digesting the history of this country since its independence. Thinking about at least some of that history would be a good thing to do during the nation's Independence Day holiday.

Of course, we'll likely be enjoying some time off – get-togethers, picnics, some travel, some fireworks. One of the reasons we have the ability to do those things is that we live in a country where freedom is so important. We have freedom to travel, to gather, to choose where we worship, and have so many other freedoms that are not enjoyed in other places in the world. Remember (and say "thanks to God") for the many freedoms we enjoy in the United States of America. They are blessings from God. While we celebrate our nation's INdependence, we should always remember our DEpendence upon a loving God.

Prayer thought: Dear God, we are blessed. You have been kind and gracious to those in the United States. While we enjoy many freedoms, let us never take them for granted and let us show to those around us our dependence upon you. In Jesus' name. Amen.

TOWARD GREAT MEMORIES

It's not a holiday, as such, but it is a significant time for many. Best wishes to all the parents, grandparents, and care givers who are now, or will soon be, sending children off to school. All of us want the best for the children.

Those of us who are older look back on school days as very good days. Sure, we had our share of concerns as young people, and at the time, those concerns may have seemed quite serious. Now, most of us think of them as wonderful times. We do so, in part, because we had strong support from parents and friends and teachers and others.

Thank God for all those who care for the students of today. You are following the example of Jesus who cared dearly for children. With the help, kindness, and support you show for the young people of today, they will one day have great memories, too.

Prayer thought: We pray at this time, loving Lord, for teachers, parents, and all those who support our children as they go off to school. Make them instruments of your care. And be with the young ones you love so much. Amen.

WITH ALL YOUR HEART

Of these two comments, which do you hear more often? One) I had a great day at work today. Or two) I had a miserable day at work today.

Number two may be heard more often. It's been said that "Work cheerfully done is usually well done." If we are not happy or satisfied with what we are doing, the task becomes a burden…and we don't feel good about doing it.

God, in the Bible, encourages us to do what we do cheerfully. *"Whatsoever you do, work at it with all your heart, as working for the Lord, not for human masters… It is the Lord Christ you are serving"* (Colossians 3:23-24 NIV).

Honest labor is a great blessing. When we have a job we can do cheerfully, we are fortunate, indeed. Today, approach your work with a sense of enthusiasm and joy. It will improve both you and the work you do.

Prayer thought: Whatever our labor may be, Lord Jesus, let us approach it with the desire to do it with an eye toward excellence. The chance to work is a gift. Move us to value it and to work as if to you. In your name. Amen.

GRAND PARENTING

I haven't been able to determine exactly how or why this date was chosen, but the first Sunday after Labor Day has been designated "Grandparents' Day." Perhaps the greeting card companies had something to do with designating another day that could spur card sales. Or, perhaps it was grandparents lobbying for some additional recognition for all they do as grandparents. After all, we have Mother's Day and Father's Day, why not a Grandparents' Day?

No matter how the day came about…and even if there were no special day on the calendar, grandparents should be saluted. They can be wonderful influences in the lives of grandchildren. Likewise, grandchildren can be wonderful sources of joy and pride for them.

Those grandparents who seek to be positive examples by living their faith in Jesus Christ truly deserve our thanks and admiration. Special thanks to all grandparents today who seek to do that!

Prayer thought: Heavenly Father, you placed us in families and knew that the older generations could be powerful caretakers and influences upon younger generations. Thank you for grandparents who improve the lives and faith of the young. In Jesus' name. Amen.

GRACE ALONE

I t was actually on this date in 1941 (October 31) that a famous United States monument was completed – Mount Rushmore. The monument features U.S. Presidents Washington, Jefferson, Lincoln, and Theodore Roosevelt.

Many Christians remember this date for another reason and for a man who has no such monument. Yet, this man helped change history. In 1517, on this date, the Protestant Reformation began when a monk by the name of Martin Luther sought to bring some insights from God's Word to people of his day. Some of those insights and many of his teachings have been powerful in helping people understand God's Word and God's plan that includes salvation through Jesus Christ.

A blessed Reformation Day to all of you. May the monument to the Reformation be in the hearts and minds of those who have benefited from a clearer understanding of God's great love and grace for all people!

Prayer thought: Your undeserved love to us, Dear God, in Jesus Christ is a message so clearly stated in your Holy Word. Keep us in the faith that acknowledges we are saved by your grace, through faith, for the sake of Jesus Christ. Amen.

SAINTS ABOVE

Perhaps this was the year a person near and dear to you died. It's painful. Yet, on this special day – the first day of November, Christians around the world remember, with thanksgiving, those faithful Christians who have died in the Lord. This All Saints Day, is a time to thank God for those saints whom He has welcomed into His eternal home.

Most of us have experienced the death of friends and loved ones. Today, and often, God would have you remember the blessings brought to you and others through the persons who have gone before. If those persons had faith in Jesus Christ, there's reason to be thankful…and even joyful…for the gift of eternal life the person has now received.

Thank God for all the saints! Thank God for the gift of faith that will enable us one day to follow those who have gone before and join with all the saints in heaven.

Prayer thought: Eternal God, you gave the gift of faith to many saints who are now eternally yours in heaven. We praise you that they kept the faith until the end. Inspire us to follow their example. In Jesus' name. Amen.

IN OUR STEAD

Every generation in the United States since the time of the Revolutionary War has experienced some type of armed conflict – more often than not on soil in other places in the world. As much as generation after generation has looked forward to a world without war, wars have persisted. And that has meant that men and women have found themselves in harm's way and many have had their lives cut short.

If you are a veteran, we express our thanks to you today for your willingness to serve in our stead. If you are the loved one of one who died in a war, we thank you for your sacrifice and for all the pain you have endured. We owe our veterans and their loved ones a lot, and we are pleased to honor you today. As we do so, we pray for God's guidance and protection in your lives.

Prayer thought: Lord God, in a world where wars and threats of wars exist, give us hearts and minds attuned to the peace only you can give. Embrace with your peace those who served in the military and those who have suffered the effects of war. In Jesus' name. Amen.

THANKS TO, AND FOR, PEOPLE

Nearly everyone is saying something today about being thankful. Some may even list a number of things for which they can be thankful. The list can be a very long one. On that list should be the people God has brought into our lives. Being thankful for special people may be among the most important thanks-givings.

It feels good when someone passes along a compliment or a word of thanks, doesn't it! Remember that and look for those around you who could use a compliment and a word of thanks today or on any day in the future.

Thankfulness is always appropriate, especially when it includes thankfulness to God for all His blessings in Jesus Christ. Among those blessings are people. If you have an opportunity today to say a special "thanks" to them and for them, do so. It could make your Thanksgiving even more meaningful and enjoyable.

Prayer thought: Loving Lord, you have brought into our lives many for whom we can be thankful. Along with all our expressions of thanksgiving for all your blessings, may we recognize the gifts of people. In Jesus' name. Amen.

BRIGHTNESS DAWNING

During the Advent season in the northern hemisphere, it's fairly common to hear people say "Boy, the hours of daylight are certainly short these days!"

If you're not fond of all the darkness at this time of the year, turn in your Bible to Psalm 34. It is a psalm of praise. Verses 17 and 18 say: *"When the righteous cry out for help, the Lord hears them and delivers them out of all their troubles. The Lord is near to the brokenhearted and saves the crushed in spirit."* That's actually an appropriate reference to Advent. The Christ whose birth we anticipate – the Light of the world – comes to brighten the dark corners of our lives, ease our troubles and assure us of a brilliant eternity.

Despite the darkness outside these days, enjoy the brightness of this Advent season. Celebrate the coming of the Light of the world who can make any day brighter!

Prayer thought: Lord Jesus, anticipating a joyful event or a special blessing can bring about feelings of wonder and hope. As we look forward to again celebrating your coming as the Christ Child, brighten our hearts and our days. In your name. Amen.

WONDER AND JOY

Among other things, you may hear people at this time of the year saying, "I can't believe it is Christmas already. Where has the past year gone?" Another thing you may hear on this particular day is something such as "This is a favorite day of the year for me." That's clearly my sentiment. What helps to make it the marvelous experience it is are the worship services with glorious music, beautiful decorations, and the song of the Angels so often repeated on Christmas Eve: *"Glory to God in the Highest, and on earth, peace, good will toward men"* (Luke 2:14 KJV). For me, it's a quiet time in the midst of a busy and hectic season to really ponder the wonder of God's love in sending Jesus Christ to earth. May God bless your Christmas Eve with a sense of wonder and joy that will last for many days to come!

Prayer thought: With your blessing, Lord Jesus, the observance of Christmas Eve can be a holy one – a chance to marvel again at the miracle of God becoming a human being. May we celebrate with all joy and sincerity your birth. In your holy name we pray. Amen.

CELEBRATE THE GIFT

A week or two before Christmas some years ago my young daughter came home and announced that we needed more outside decorations. We simply had a spotlight shining on a wreath that was hanging on the side of the house. "It's embarrassing," she said. "Can't we do more lights, or something?"

Competition, I thought. So we always have to be in competition with everyone around us? But then I had another thought. Maybe it wasn't competition at all. Maybe it was the thought that we weren't expressing well enough how special Christmas is.

For Christians, Christmas is a true highlight of the year. It's the birth of a Savior, Jesus Christ, the promise of life forever, the assurance that God really loves us that much. And why not some special expressions of the joy we feel. Maybe it's a few more lights. We truly do have a reason to celebrate the great miracle of Christmas.

Prayer thought: The angels announced it to us, too – "For unto you is born this day…a Savior, who is Christ the Lord" (Luke 2:11). We celebrate your birth, Lord Jesus, and pray we might live in that sense of celebration in all we do. In your holy name. Amen.

ENDINGS AND BEGINNINGS

The calendar suggests that today is a very special day – the end of something…and that tomorrow will be the beginning of something. Without what the calendar suggests, this would likely be just another day and tomorrow would be, too. On this day that leads us to think of the past and wonder about the future, an appropriate idea might be to look at life – no matter what day it is – as a true gift.

If we could just be reminded frequently that life is indeed a gift, our problems and uncertainties would likely seem less severe and finding solutions to the challenges we face would be easier. We all have our share of problems. As we look ahead to the new year, let's remind ourselves that life is a gift from a loving Heavenly Father. Remembering that frequently throughout the new year could help us enjoy and appreciate it a whole lot more.

Prayer thought: For the ways you have touched our lives with your grace and mercy in the year gone by, Heavenly Father, we thank you. Fill our lives in the new year to come with your presence. In Jesus' name. Amen.

LET IT BE SO

A CLOSING AMEN

A very well known radio preacher by the name of Oswald Hoffman, who is now sainted, would frequently end his Gospel messages with a statement similar to this: "And what else is there to say, but Amen!"

"Amen" is a little word with a simple, but significant, meaning. It is more than a word to signal the end of a prayer or hymn. "Amen" means "let it be so." When Christians pray in the name of Jesus Christ and end their prayers with that little word, they know that, according to God's plans, there is the Almighty power capable of answering the prayer. The simple word "Amen" is an expression of faith that says to Jesus Christ, "I am confident – especially because of your victory on Easter – that You can answer this prayer, and if it be Your will, LET IT BE SO! It means that all Christians can pray with faith and confidence. Yes they can! AMEN!

Prayer thought: When we pray in your name, Lord Jesus, let it be so. Let your name be praised and your will be done. Let your plans be accomplished. Let your blessing be upon us. Amen…and amen!

THANK YOU

For all your prayers, and all you do in Jesus' name,

LET IT BE SO!

Thank you for sharing in these
BY THE WAY messages!